MY LIFE: HERE AND THERE

MY LIFE: HERE AND THERE

A Journey that Transcends Time and Space

ROBERT GINSBERG

Waterside Productions

ISBN-13: 978-1-958848-98-2 print edition
ISBN-13: 978-1-958848-99-9 e-book edition

Waterside Productions
2055 Oxford Ave
Cardiff, CA 92007
www.waterside.com

TABLE OF CONTENTS

INTRODUCTION

We are all used to reading biographies of high-profile people from the present and the past. Although I have a bit of media presence, I am not recognizable, and not a famous actor, politician, artist, musician, or athlete. I am someone who has lived a life filled with a mixture of profound sadness and joy, and for the last twenty years has been seeking answers to life's big questions. This book is a biographical novel that I hope will evoke emotion and provoke thought. You may laugh and cry when reading the factual account of my life, but a twist in the story will hopefully answer things that you have pondered over the years.

As the co-founder of Forever Family Foundation, a global not-for-profit organization, over the years I have met and interviewed hundreds of scientists, researchers, medical doctors, academics, and mediums who believe that our consciousness survives our physical death. Their belief is not based upon blind faith or religion, but evidence. Unlike my first non-fiction book, *The Medium Explosion*, this book is not meant to inform readers about such evidence. Instead, this work is to entertain and hopefully inspire others who may relate to my journey in this life.

Baby Boomers like myself who grew up in the fifties and sixties will certainly relate to many of the things they read here, but my hope is that newer generations, in addition to being entertained, will gain additional wisdom, and start to contemplate meaning and purpose. I find that people in this world fall into two camps. You may believe that your life, despite free will, is pre-determined and that there are no coincidences. Or you may maintain that your life is random and chaotic, and things just happen with no order. However, what I find with increased urgency today is that more people of all beliefs are starting to question their own mortality. This is understandable, as we live in fear of wars, pandemics, mass murders, global warming, famine, discrimination, and erosion of human rights.

If you believe that life is extinguished forever when we die, as I did for most of my life, there are not many incentives to live a life filled with empathy, compassion, and love. On the other hand, if you believe that life continues in another dimension, and the way in which we navigate our life affects us in other realms, there is such an incentive. I speak of this not in the context of blind faith preached by organized religion, but in a broader evidence based spiritual sense dominated by self-judgment.

For two decades I rarely talked in public about my personal life, as our focus was simply to help others. However, after we were featured in the Netflix series Surviving Death, I came to realize that my story was worth telling, and I hope that you will agree. I apologize in advance for some "off-color" language and content but growing up in the inner city instilled such things in my psyche and influenced my personality and somewhat raw sense of humor.

THE DAY THAT CHANGED
MY LIFE FOREVER

It was approximately 3:00AM on the morning of September 1, 2002, and I was awakened by my wife Phran sitting up in bed. She was silent, but trembling and ashen white, and I asked her what was wrong but received no answer. After a little while I asked again. She did not look at me, continued her blank gaze straight ahead, and said "Something horrible is going to happen today."

"What does that mean, what is going to happen?"

"I can't tell you exactly. I just know that it will be utterly devastating and change our lives forever."

I considered myself to be a left-brained logical thinker and would be the first to tell you that things such as visions or precognition defy mainstream science and were therefore not possible. However, I remembered that in our years together there were several instances where she had such precognitive moments. They were good things, but all played out exactly the way she described, so logic told me that if she were right then, she could be right now.

I decided to take this seriously and kept tabs on my three children throughout the day. My oldest child, Jonathan, was preparing to return to the University of Delaware the following day. We were packing our SUV, filling every crevice with his stuff while Phran supervised using her superior geometric reasoning skills. My middle child, Kori, had already started her college career the week before and was settling in at Carnegie Mellon University. I dropped my youngest child, Bailey, off in town at her part-time job,

1

her last day of work before she returned to Cold Spring Harbor High School, a place she adored.

The day was going well, and as Phran's vision faded from my awareness, I decided that we should meet in town for dinner. I picked up Bailey from her job in our little two-seater sports car because our SUV was packed and ready to go, while Phran and Jon took our sedan to meet us at the restaurant. Bailey and Phran were having a conversation at dinner, but I was talking to Jon and didn't hear what they were saying. I found out years later that Bailey was upset, as she told Phran that she and her best friend decided to visit a palm reader in town. Bailey was told that she had a very short lifeline, which Bailey took seriously and found distressing. Despite this, we all had a nice dinner and waited for the restaurant owner to come over to say hello. We were there so often that we were always greeted and given a special dessert, but for some reason, on this day, he never stopped by. I asked for the check, and we made plans to drive home. Phran mentioned that we needed a couple of food essentials and suggested that I return home in our sedan with Jon and Bailey, and she would stop at the "drive-up" store and meet us at home. That seemed like an odd suggestion, and I dismissed it, telling her that there was no reason for her to drive alone. Instead, I sent Jon to drive Bailey home in the sports car with instructions to continue getting ready for school. Meanwhile, Phran and I picked up the groceries and headed home.

We lived in a rural area, with only one road in and out. As we neared home, we saw that a serious accident had occurred, and two cars were on the side of the road. Phran started screaming and I said, "it's not them; it's not them." As we got closer and realized that it was our car that was demolished, panic, disbelief, and horror unfolded. Our car had been hit broadside where Bailey was sitting. Bailey was unconscious and Jon was thrashing about wildly. I pulled out my phone to dial 911, but phone service in our area was spotty and the call would not go through, and I must have tried calling fifty times. We were about twenty minutes from the nearest town, so I knew that even if I reached 911, we had a long wait for help. I

was screaming for help at the top of my lungs while Phran tried
to attend to the kids, but there was nobody to hear my screams.
Everything was a blur. This could not be happening. I realized that
the accident site was in front of an historic landmark where a wedding was taking place in the barn. I think that I ran there asking for
help, but I am not sure.

I remember another car stopping and letting us know that he
got through to 911 and help was on the way. He announced that he
was a respiratory therapist and tried to do what he could, although
he had no equipment. I saw his face as he looked at Bailey, and
complete panic set in. A police car eventually showed up, but inexplicably the car contained no basic first aid or life saving devices,
and it took twenty-two minutes for an ambulance to arrive. Phran
went in the ambulance with Bailey to Huntington Hospital, while
Jon was airlifted to another hospital with severe brain injuries. The
local police officer drove me to that hospital, a drive that was torturous and surreal.

I sat in the waiting room wanting to crawl out of my skin. I was
waiting for word about Bailey at the other hospital, and information
regarding the extent of Jon's injuries. The possibility of losing two
children was inconceivable, and I paced and trembled, not knowing
whether to pray to or curse the universe. After what seemed like an
eternity but was probably an hour or two, I was told I had a phone
call. As I picked up the hospital phone, I saw the hospital chaplain
standing before me. I screamed into the phone "no, do not tell me
that my daughter is dead....do not tell me that!" When I heard "we
did everything we could" I dropped the phone and ran outside to
try to breathe before I died.

A few hours later, Phran joined me at the hospital. I don't know
how she got there, but she did. Before her arrival Jon's doctor met
with me and advised that Jon had significant brain injuries and was
in a coma. Other than that, he could not tell me if Jon would wake
up, and what the permanent effects of the brain injury would be if
he did survive. I sat there in total shock and disbelief, entrenched
in a world that was not recognizable. Hours ago, we were having

a nice family gathering, and in the blink of an eye my precious daughter was gone, and I might lose my son as well. This was simply not possible, and I would not accept it. Words seem silly and woefully inadequate to describe the horror and devastation, as the life force was forcibly drained from my being.

I remember that when Phran walked into the hospital we fell into each other's arms, squeezing tightly with tears streaming down our faces. It was as if being wrapped in her cocoon-like embrace would make reality go away. Much of what happened next is a blur, but apparently someone ushered us upstairs to a waiting room where we sat vigil for Jonathan. Oddly enough, despite my hazy memory, what I remember most is going to the bathroom every five minutes to urinate as shock evidently wreaks havoc on your bodily functions. I don't remember how long we sat there, but sometime the next day we decided that Phran needed to go back home to make funeral arrangements for Bailey. After that, Phran and I took shifts so that one of us would be always there.

After Bailey's funeral, while friends and family gathered at our home, I rushed back to the hospital, sitting at Jon's bedside. Jon's girlfriend at the time also sat with Jon, as did her father, who talked incessantly to Jon on the assumption that he would somehow hear him. Sometime that afternoon, on the day we buried his sister, we saw Jon's eyes flutter, followed by his awakening. His first words were to his girlfriend's dad, "You are a pain in the ass," to which the dad responded that those words were music to his ears. I remember trying to engage Jon in conversation to gauge what damage had occurred that might be permanent. I knew he would heal from the surgery to repair his shattered eye socket, but the rest was a mystery. One of the doctors told me that he was cautiously optimistic, but Jon would require months of therapy in a facility that deals with brain injuries.

Meanwhile, Jon had no memory of the accident, which I suppose was a blessing, and we did not know how and when we should tell him. Upon Jon's release from the hospital, it was determined that he could have his daily therapy as an out-patient, and I would drop him off at the facility every morning, and Phran would pick him up at the end of the day. While our lives were in utter devastation and profound sadness, we were encouraged by the progress that Jon was making. He was my focus because that was what had to be, but I did not see any way of surviving the death of Bailey, and every night I wished that I would die.

After several months, when it became clear that Jon was going to make a complete recovery and return to college, I suddenly remembered the morning of the accident. How did Phran know? I became obsessed with trying to find out how it was possible to have such knowledge. In my mind there were two possible explanations. Either Phran had a precognitive moment where she was able to catch a glimpse of the future, or somebody was sending her a warning message. I realized that the source of that message could have been from a living or a discarnate entity. Not only did I need to find out how it was possible, but I also needed to know if there was any hope that my daughter still survived in some form. In other words, was there evidence that our consciousness, or mind, or soul separated from our physical bodies and continued in a different dimension? I met with medical doctors and scientists across the country that studied consciousness and I read hundreds upon hundreds of books. What I discovered was astounding, and I will discuss a bit of this in later chapters.

THE BEGINNING

I grew up in Brooklyn, New York in a working-class family. My father toiled alongside his father and brothers in Manhattan making fur coats for retailers and wholesalers. I shudder at this occupation now, but back then I didn't give it much thought. As a contractor he didn't make much money, but we never went without and lived a comfortable life. Dad used to leave the house at 5:30AM every morning, including most Saturdays, and didn't arrive back home until 8PM. Occasionally, on days off from school or on weekends, I used to accompany him to work in the "shop", and my ass was dragging by midafternoon. I then decided such labor would not be for me when I grew up, but my admiration grew for the sacrifices made by my dad for his family. My mother worked various part time and full-time jobs, in addition to periods of simply being a "housewife." My brother Barry is almost four years younger than me, and the family was astonished when he was born with red hair. That, of course, triggered an endless stream of comments such as "Where did the red hair come from"? The answer was always the same, whether it came from one of us or the questioner, "the milkman." Yes, in those days almost every home had a metal milk box placed outside their door, and glass milk bottles were delivered regularly.

My long-term memory is terrible, but there are certain things that I do recall, such as when I started school, it was decided that I would begin in first grade and bypass kindergarten. I don't know what the teachers were thinking, as what kind of aptitude test do you give a four-year-old? In any event, I began my school career a year younger than my fellow students. Since to this day I have terrible geometric reasoning skills, whenever I did something stupid my wife would respond with "of course, you skipped kindergarten!"

I would walk to elementary school every day, a healthy distance from home but it took no more than twenty minutes. There was a candy store a block away from school, so on the days that I managed to scrounge a few pennies together I looked forward to securing some treats. Back then we had no backpacks and simply carried our books under our arms, and I remember that when I reached school and unloaded my books it took a while for my arm to straighten out.

School always came easy to me, and I was often bored, which usually spelled trouble. One incident in third grade has never faded from my memory. In those days, each class had a long closet with assigned hooks for students to hang up their coats. I got into an argument with a girl in the class (me being the self-appointed leader of the "I hate girls club" didn't help the situation), and the girl insisted that I was infringing upon her hook. My reply was a resounding "fuck you!" It was then that the girl started a slow march, a journey that seemed to take forever, up to the front of the class and said, "Miss Taub, Robert Ginsberg just said "fuck you." I was always on good terms with my teachers, and her disappointed and shocked stare hurt me. I was asked to apologize and did so, but the apology was more to appease the teacher than the student. At the end of third grade my parents were asked for permission to have me "skipped" from third to fifth grade. Skipping grades was often a bad idea for the student, and thankfully my parents declined. In addition to the gap in knowledge, this would have made me two years younger than my classmates.

Several things stand out for me when I try to recall the ages of seven to ten. One frightening experience occurred when our pediatrician prescribed some sort of Sulphur compound for me, which I now assume was to act as an antibiotic. My mother misread the dosage, which had profound consequences, as I began to experience hallucinations, including seeing orange darts shooting out from the ceiling, and seeing snakes under my pillow. My parents attributed my claims to an active imagination, but I was scared and angry that they would not believe me and thought that I might be going crazy. This lasted for quite a while, even after the medication was eventually stopped, but in time it went away.

Another time I was home sick, and our doctor was summoned. This concept must seem strange to the newer generations, but back then the doctor would come to you! He would arrive with his black doctor's bag that appeared to contain everything imaginable relating to medicine. On this occasion Dr. Nathan announced that he needed to give me an injection, but I hated needles and wasn't having any part of this. While he was preparing the syringe, I retreated to my bedroom, and since the door to my bedroom did not lock, I mustered all my strength to move a heavy wooden dresser in front of the door. Knocks on my door began, as well as pleas for me to come out, which turned into not so veiled threats from my mom, who was seething at this point. Nope, my decision was made, and Dr. Nathan left the premises. I don't know what made my mother angrier, having to pay for the visit or the fact that I was untreated.

In my family my mother was the disciplinarian and my father the good guy. Punishment was quite different back then, as when my mom lost her temper over something that I did, the strap would come out. This was simply a man's belt, including the metal buckle. My rear end was the target, and she would wail away unmercifully until I either gave in, or she tired, and I would try not to give her the satisfaction of screaming unless it was absolutely necessary. She would often say, "You wait until your father comes home!" to which I replied, "No, *you* wait until dad comes home!" Dad would walk in the door and the poor guy would be verbally assaulted by mom yelling about everything I did wrong, however, inevitably, dad would almost always take my side. This would drive mom up a wall, and then my father would bear the brunt, usually in the form of silent treatment. My father rarely disciplined me for anything, however, all he had to do was look at me with disappointment, and that look would bother me immensely. What parents got away with then would get them arrested today, but corporal punishment was considered good parenting at that time. Of course, getting hit with the belt did absolutely nothing to change my behavior, and, if anything, did the opposite. But one stare from dad would do the trick, a valuable lesson that followed me into my adult years.

As a child, I distinctly remember a pervasive feeling that I was the only human being on Earth, and everyone in my life were simply robot-like actors. My parents and brother were evidently best suited for the roles they played. Yeah, I was a weird kid. I suppose that a psychologist would have a field day with these thoughts and attribute them to feelings of isolation, being different, or not quite fitting in. I am sure that science fiction fans might say that I could have been right, but I think not. There are those who say that the physical world is the dream world, and what comes after is our true home. Perhaps I had insight into this, but at least I prefer to think of it in this manner.

. I enjoyed my early years in school but could not wait to get home at the end of each school day. It obviously wasn't to go to a computer or play video games. No, that is when the endless fun would begin in the street. We lived on a block of approximately fifty attached brick two-story, two-family homes on each side of the street, and the block was a city within itself, with virtually all my friends within two hundred feet of my home. When we wanted to get a game going, we started "calling on" our friends, which meant ringing doorbells to ask if so and so can come out to play. In view of the proliferation of smart devices entertaining us today, it is simply amazing how many games we were able to play in the fifties and sixties with so few tools. To play football in the street there was no getting around it, as a football was needed, but that was all. The minimum number of people for a football game would be three, a quarterback, receiver, and defensive player. The more people we had, the more elaborate the game would become. A typical play that would be called in the huddle was a down and out, and the *out* meant between two parked cars. Occasionally, one of us would get impaled on one of those huge Cadillac tail fins, but that was part of the game. We didn't pay much attention to injuries when we played our sports, as all our focus was on winning the game. Of course, there was that rare time when we suspended the game for about fifteen minutes. Our friend Philip's mom came out of her house to start yelling for Philip to immediately come inside, as he was in deep trouble for something. About two minutes later Philip came running out of the house screaming, with the tip of a high-heeled shoe sticking out of his head. Yep, his mom must have been *really* pissed off. We knew enough not to simply pull out the shoe, and Philip's uncle took him to a doctor, with his head still connected to the shoe. Ten minutes later our game resumed, and a stitched Philip returned to our games about two days later.

One day a boy named Roland came by our football game and asked if he could play. We had never seen him before, and it turned out that he lived in an old home just beyond our development. We didn't know if he went to school, and if so, it certainly wasn't ours. His home must have been well over one hundred years old and provided a sharp contrast to the cookie cutter modern homes that lined our street. Roland started inviting us over to his home while his dad was working and was very generous in giving us snacks. I recall his dad coming home early one day, and he was not happy when he saw his son was wasting his hard-earned money on giving away food, and to the "rich kids" no less. I guess because we lived in new homes the assumption was that we were wealthy. There were several cool things about Roland's house. The basement was creepy and filled with all sorts of interesting tools and artifacts, and outside there was an unused little room attached to the garage. We made that our private clubhouse, decorated it accordingly, and many schemes were hatched in that tiny oasis, our own domain and escape to a world hidden from outside reality. However, the best thing about Roland's house is that it had a field of grass on the side of the home, not the tiny patches of sod that we all had in front of our homes, but a huge expanse of nature. To us, that meant football field. We would don our shoulder pads and helmets and play *rough tackle* football, real football. When we played in the street each play ended when we touched our opponent with two hands, but here we got to play out our fantasies and work out our aggression. In our crew there was little Stevie, short and skinny but possessing an iron will. Then there was Big Steve, tall and athletic, and it seemed that little Stevie didn't have a chance. However, little Stevie had mastered the art of tackling, and every time that he chopped down his huge opponent, we would all shriek with glee.

When the weather was simply too cold to play outside, unless of course there was snow to play with, my brother and I entertained ourselves indoors. When it snowed, sledding became a competition. Every home on the block shared one driveway that led to the garages at the back of each home. To turn into the common driveway, one had to go down a fairly steep hill, and, considering that we lived in an area where hills were non-existent, that ramp became Mount Everest to us. It wasn't enough for us to simply enjoy sledding down the hill, as we insisted on turning each slide down as a competition, and the one whose sled covered the most distance won.

How we managed to survive those years is beyond me, but perhaps it toughened us up, not that my brother needed to be tougher. Despite being younger he was taller and stronger and had the reputation in the neighborhood as a bully. Although I never witnessed it, supposedly all the mothers on the block had a warning system, as they would knock on doors or start calling each other letting them know that Barry was on the loose. I think the stories have been embellished over the years, but there is no doubt that there was an issue. Oddly enough, he grew up to be the total opposite, kind, compassionate, and loving.

Indoor activities usually took place in our full basement in the house, a space that also housed the washer, dryer, and provided storage for various other household essentials. It had a tiled concrete floor, but that did not stop my brother and I from playing *rough tackle*, just he against me. A football was not practical, so we used a pair of rolled up socks. If we wanted to pass instead of run, we had to pass it to ourselves, flinging the socks and being agile enough to run and catch it before it landed. Being tackled on concrete is not fun, so we would do everything humanly possible to avoid being slammed to the ground.

Outdoor activities became our own insulated world, the sporting games were varied, and we often improvised regarding required equipment. Stickball required either a broom stick or a store-bought stickball bat. There were two types of rubber balls, each having distinct properties. Spalding balls were lighter and could be hit further but would often split in half if hit extremely hard, whereas Pensy Pinkies were more durable and lasted longer. When we played stickball one person always pitched, which meant we also needed a catcher and at least one fielder. Our scoring system was unique to city kids. The street had round sewer covers that were placed about every one-hundred feet apart. If you hit a ball that was not caught and landed before the first sewer, that was a single. Hitting between the first and second sewers meant a double. Hitting between the second and third sewers was a triple, and a monster shot that traveled three sewers was a home run. When meeting a new player, the first question asked was "how many sewers can you hit?" I can't imagine that question being received the same way in the suburbs.

My fondest memories involving stickball were the bonding that took place in my family. On Sunday, my dad would drive my brother and me to a special school yard. This school had a u-shaped courtyard, where two four story buildings were separated by about one hundred feet, which made it perfect for stickball. Each floor of the building had caged in windows, and boxes were painted on one wall, designating the strike zone. We took turns hitting, pitching, and fielding. A hit above the first set of windows was a single, second set a double, third set a triple and top window was a home run. The fielder could catch the rebound off the wall, and if successful the batter was out. One day we invited one of the block's young dads to join our game, and about five minutes in, one of us hit a screaming line drive that our newcomer tried to catch, and it broke his finger. We didn't know it was broken until later, so we insisted that he continue playing in the game. That day a new term entered our stickball vocabulary, as *fingerbreaker* became the term used to describe an exceedingly hard-hit ball. It was endless fun, after which we would race to the car where dad would drive to Kwik-Burger, where he would buy a bag of burgers and three vanilla shakes. The burgers were fifteen cents each and the shakes a quarter, and we dined like kings for about two bucks. Those games were the happiest memory of my childhood, pure joy, not a care in the world, and represented a bond that can never be broken.

One of the downsides to playing stickball on our street was that fouls balls were lost on the common roofs to our left and right. However, every couple of months one of us would enlist our dad's help in a much-anticipated ball retrieving adventure. A ladder would be placed on our small second floor terrace, and we then would be able to climb up to the roof. About every fifteen homes there were ten-foot alleys that separated one section from the rest. That meant that in each section we had roof access to all fifteen homes, which usually resulted in a treasure chest recovery of at least thirty balls. We rarely had to buy more balls.

With those same balls we could play a bunch of different sidewalk games. There was *box ball*, where you and your opponent each defended the box in front of them. The goal is to hit the ball in the other person's box, without letting it bounce twice before hitting it back. *Hit the penny* was a game where a penny was placed on the crack that separated two concrete slabs. Two players, facing each other, took turns in trying to bounce the ball off the penny. A strike was worth one point, but if the penny flipped over it was a two-pointer. There was also a game where two players had five boxes between them. A player would try to throw the ball to the box immediately in front of his opponent. If that was successful, the goal was to bounce the ball once in the second box and the first, and so on, until a player was able to hit all five boxes, with no more than one bounce per box. *Stoop ball* was an interesting game, but first you needed to locate a stoop with five or six steps. The player throws the ball against the steps and tries to catch the rebound. Catch it after it bounces, one point. Catch it on a fly, two points. The games were endless, free, competitive, and entertaining.

On school days we would break for dinner and then return to the games until it became too dark to see. We watched out for each other, as one of us would always yell out "car!" when we saw a car approaching us from either direction. There were a few close calls when a vehicle would sneak up on us, usually attributed to either driver inattentiveness or malicious intent. During these years I also became introduced to gambling. All of us had extensive collections of baseball cards, and when we weren't trading the cards, we would engage in several different card activities. *Flipping* involved a player releasing a card to the floor in a rotating fashion. The card would land on either the photo side, or the stats side. The other participant would then flip his card, trying to match the correct side. If he did match, he wins the card, and if not, he loses his card. We would usually flip the cards in a series, so multiple cards were won or lost. Another card game was flinging your card against a wall. The person who flung his card closest to the wall won the card, and we also played this game with real coins.

I had hundreds upon hundreds of baseball cards, some very collectible. My mother, during one of her clearing out projects, decided to throw out my old dresser, including all the cards that were housed within, and I would estimate that today's value of those cards would be in the thousands. I also collected coins and stamps, and my brother and I had coin books, a place to house the coins by year and mint. My father used to stop at the bank and bring home rolls of coins, and it was great fun to find ones that we needed. I kept all my rare coins in the top drawer of my desk, until one day my brother wanted a pop from the ice cream truck but had no money. He found my hidden treasure and bought his ice cream, and that fifteen cents treat cost me about one hundred and fifty dollars.

I owe my introduction into the world of business to our next-door neighbor, who had a superette on wheels. Bill's Superette was a grocery and candy store on wheels, a huge van lined with a shelving system and stocked with grocery essentials and a large variety of candy. Bill's garage was his warehouse, and he would hire us kids to stock the truck and assist him on his rounds throughout the neighborhood. Opening cartons of canned goods was tedious work, but the cartons of delectable candy bars were almost too much to handle, as the temptation to sneak a few bars was always present. Bill never paid us in money, candy was his currency, and as far as we were concerned, we saw nothing wrong with our compensation. One day on his route he trusted me with giving the customers their orders, announcing the total due, and then taking the money and making change where applicable. It was a welcome variation from stocking goods, and I saw this as a promotion. Things were going smoothly until one of the transactions got complicated. I don't know whether it was by design on the part of the customer to shortchange me, but she kept adjusting the quantities of the order and requesting additional items. I got totally confused and was not sure that I provided the correct amount of change. After the route was over, Bill always reconciled the day's receipts against inventory, and he told me that I was short five dollars. I could not tell if he was accusing me of pocketing the extra cash or admonishing me for being so careless with his money, but either way I felt terrible. It wasn't about the missing cash that troubled me most, but the fact that I let it happen. I was good at math, and this was an abject failure on my part. I also did not appreciate Bill's accusatory tone with me, and I was super angry when he refused to pay me my candy when the day ended. That was the last day that I worked for Bill, but the experience did teach me a lesson about keeping my wits about me when dealing with money, especially the money of others.

It was fifth grade where all the students were one day herded into the auditorium, where we would be given a music aptitude test to determine who would be eligible to join the school orchestra. To my knowledge I had no ability or aptitude for playing a musical instrument, but I was good at taking tests and somehow managed to pass, and I was told to report to the school conductor the following day. I was asked what instrument I would like to try, but I had no preference, so the saxophone was selected for me. My mother had to take me to a music store for me to rent a saxophone, which

I would have to bring with me to school on the long walk. The conductor gave me a little instruction, but I was advised that private lessons would be needed, which I subsequently took, practiced religiously, and I still sucked. I kept at it and made no progress. Some kids down the block, kids that didn't play sports with us, were forming a band. They heard I played the saxophone, so they invited me to come jam with them. After thirty minutes of torture to their eardrums, they told me to leave, and I gladly complied.

The conductor eventually gave up and decided that I should be assigned a different instrument, a clarinet. Another rental, more lessons, and I was still atrocious. You would think that, at this point, the conductor would have realized that test or no test, this kid has no musical ability, but no, and it was on to the next instrument, a flute. Same story. The only people happy with my playing were the owners of the music store, as I was their best customer. There was a brief fling with the tuba, and we won't even discuss that. The last attempt was the trombone. I hated to fail at anything, and I decided to put all my efforts into making this strange contraption emit pleasant sounds. We rented my trombone, started lessons, and I really tried hard to make it work, and I finally got to the point where I could play a rudimentary tune.

The school year was ending, and that meant the school concert for our orchestra. Every parent would be in attendance, the room would be filled, and considerable expectations would reside in the hearts of not only the parents, but the conductor. The day arrived, and as I put on my white shirt, red tie, and black pants, I was ready to shine. I was one of three trombonists, so chances are that even if I missed a note nobody would notice. The first piece that we performed included a solo with the orchestra's most talented musician, a flutist, and while she was playing her heavenly solo, I decided to clear out my trombone. Trombones have a *spit valve* that you could open to blow out the excess fluid that accumulates in the instrument. This is usually done silently, however, I was not even good at that. As the soloist reached her most thrilling moment, a resounding baritone fart released itself into the atmosphere for all to hear.

The conductor seethed and looked at me with eyes that pierced my soul. The audience was aghast, although I did hear laughter, just saying. And thus, my musical career came crashing down with a thud heard round the world.

In nineteen sixty-three my dad took me to my first baseball game at the Polo Grounds in New York City. The New York Mets, an expansion team, started their journey on these hollow grounds, as did the New York Yankees and New York Giants in the past. We were to see Sandy Koufax pitch against the Mets, and he was one of the best pitchers in the game. Up to this point, my experience of watching and rooting for my favorite team was peering at fuzzy images on a fifteen-inch black and white television, and when we made it to our seats, I was awe struck. The huge expanse of grass was greener than I could have imagined, and I had never been in a place before among so many people. The energy in the crowd was palpable, my senses were on overload, and I could hardly contain my excitement. Our seats were right behind home plate, and when Sandy threw his first pitch, a blazing fastball that hit the catcher's glove with an explosive pop, I knew that this reality was far from what I could have imagined. Despite my youthful age I began to realize that so many things in life are perceived in ways that are filtered by our experience and environment. Watching baseball on a small screen was linear, as if all the action was contained by that small tube, but being at the live game enabled you to absorb and become part of the action. In a similar fashion in life, pigeon-hole views are often mistaken for our true reality, when so much more lies beyond.

Many kids are fortunate to have a favorite uncle, and in my case, it was Uncle Joe. He never had kids of his own but loved to play with his nieces and nephews, something that we enjoyed immensely. Joe was one of those larger-than-life characters who lived life outside the box and would do things that our parents would never consider. He would take me on adventures, just the two of us, including baseball game excursions, and I treasured our time together. I remember being in our living room and seeing grim faces on both my parents, who then told me that Uncle Joe has died from a heart attack. For the first time in my young life, I was stunned, shocked, and could not fathom what I just heard. I had never lost someone that I loved, and this news hit me like a ton of bricks. I could not imagine how someone so vibrant and full of life could simply cease to exist, and it made no sense, especially considering that he had taken me to a ball game the week before. I sat in stunned silence at the news, reasoning that this must be a mistake and could not possibly be true. Reality eventually took hold and allowed me to mourn his passing, but it changed my thinking about life and those who surround us. I was no longer the care-free kid that I was before, and a certain fear of the future started to take hold.

As I now reflect upon those early years there are a few observations that are meaningful to mention. All my friends were competitive as hell, but we saw no color or race. Sport was sport, and if you could play you were one of us. We had little down time despite the lack of material possessions. We used our minds to create what we needed, something that I now appreciate considering today's age of instant information, smart devices, and limitless forms of entertainment. In addition, instead of sitting on our asses for much of the day in front of screens, we had a healthier lifestyle by remaining physically active.

SMART DOESN'T MEAN GROWN UP

It was a bit scary graduating from elementary school and moving on to parts unknown, and a new Junior High School was just built, where I was to be in the first class at this facility. At the end of sixth grade my parents were asked permission to put me in an SP class in Junior High. I'm not sure what SP stood for, but I assume it was Special Placement, and the criteria used were teacher recommendations and standardized IQ testing. This meant that the program would compress three years of school into two. Instead of going to High School like everyone else in ninth grade, I would stay in this Junior High program for two years, and then enter High School in tenth grade. I was now old enough that my parents asked my opinion. I realized that this would make me two years younger than my classmates in High School and College, but that didn't faze me at the time. Besides, school was boring, and this might be a chance to enhance my learning, so I agreed.

The school principal did what I thought was an irresponsible thing when he greeted our class on the first day. He announced that the IQ range in the class was one hundred twenty-five to one hundred seventy-four. This fostered all sorts of issues, as for two years my classmates in the program were constantly trying to figure out who had the one hundred seventy-four, and more than a few felt inadequate. This program turned out to be a rude awakening for me, as not only did I find it difficult, but for the first time in my life I was struggling in some subjects. I hated advanced calculus, physics, and anything else that involved geometric and spatial reasoning. My brain didn't work that way, and my frustration was palpable.

I found myself being picked on by my teachers constantly, often embarrassing me in class. As I now reflect on this, I wonder if I was on the lower end of the scale and the teachers felt I needed a push to keep up, or, on the other hand, maybe I was on the upper end and the teachers were trying to get me to live up to expectations. Either way, I think that taking part in this experiment appeared to be a mistake. I did manage to get through it successfully with high grades, but I had to work my ass off in the process.

The total experience was not unlike my Little League baseball days. I was usually the best player on my team and would make the All-Star team, which would travel to play other All-Star teams from other leagues. The first time I did this I felt totally overmatched, as the opposing pitcher was six feet tall and had a beard. Yeah, thirteen years old my ass! I wouldn't be surprised if he smoked a cigar after the game while drinking a beer with his girlfriend. Gradually I learned to step up my game with hard work and much practice and was able to compete on that level. Perhaps the school experience also spurred me to achieve more in life.

So, off to High School I went, a pimply fourteen-year-old with no specific aspirations other than becoming a professional baseball player. The school was immense, housed thousands of students, and felt more like a prison than a place of learning. If I recall correctly, on my first day there the school was teeming with police officers, as someone had set off explosives in the school offices. Once again, I felt out of my league. My three years in High School are a total blur, as if I stepped into the twilight zone and those years were erased from my memory. One of my only memories is the vendor who parked his cart by the school entrance every morning. Mama's knishes were manna from heaven, round delectable treats with a soft potato inside, surrounded by the perfect envelope of crust. The metal saltshaker provided the extra taste that was needed. Whenever I had enough money, Mama provided my breakfast.

I found my high school years to be awkward. I was not outgoing and meeting new people did not come easily. I was interested in girls but didn't quite know how to make that happen. I think I went on one date during those years, and that was more like hanging out with a girl while she was babysitting. I do remember her being aggressive with me and wanting to have sex, but I wasn't all that attracted to her and didn't let it get far. Besides, I wasn't sure that I knew what to do, and I didn't have any condoms.

Every year my parents rented a summer bungalow in the Catskills of New York. It was a tradition upheld by many families at the time, especially among the Jewish community. When I was young, I would stay the entire summer in the bungalow colony with my mother and brother, but my dad had to work, so he would come join us every weekend. My brother and I kept ourselves entertained playing various sports, but we each had our own sets of friends, I remember having a crush on one girl, but she had a boyfriend and paid little attention to me. Another girl was extremely interested in me, and although she was smart, personable, and attractive, I didn't share her desire for us to become more than friends. Eventually that made her (and her parents) very angry, and she found happiness elsewhere. I don't know why I was so picky, as it wasn't as if I was God's gift to women, but I had unrealistic expectations and was seeking the perfect match.

The Catskills was the place where I smoked my first joint. Heck, it was the sixties and even my mother and her friends were toking it up occasionally. There was frequent gambling that took place in this environment, and I was too young to join any of the poker games, but my dad looked forward to playing cards most of the weekend. Monticello Racetrack was close by, and I loved going there, as my dad would buy me a racing program and I would spend time with him handicapping the horses. He would place bets for me, and I loved the action.

I remember one of the guys my age announced that he and his brother had bows and arrows, and they were going to lead us on a hunting expedition in the woods, the target being deer. I had never given any thought to hunting at the time, as the most wildlife we ever saw in Brooklyn were squirrels and rats. If it weren't for cartoons, I probably wouldn't have been able to distinguish a cow from a moose. I gave no thought to the repercussions of killing another living thing, and the prospect sounded sort of thrilling in a weird way. As someone who now abhors hunting for sport, I wonder how I could have had such insensitivity at the time, but I chalk it up to adolescent ignorance. Thankfully, the hunters were terrible at their craft, and the one deer spotted did not come within one hundred feet of his stalker's arrows.

I now realize the attraction of being away in the bungalows, especially for my parents. It was their escape from the doldrums of work and monotony of everyday life. There were no schedules, no obligations, and few worries. They had their friends, entertainment, gambling, drinking, swimming, and endless fun. They got to be kids again. I could not appreciate it back then from a kid's perspective, but I can now see how important it was for their mental health.

JUST A KID IN COLLEGE

During the last part of my senior year in high school it was time for my guidance counselor to help me pick a college and bearing in mind that the school was so huge, I didn't exactly get personal attention in this endeavor. He asked me if had an idea of what my major would be, and I definitively said "journalism," but also told him that cost would be a factor, as I would be taking out loans. I applied to about five schools, some with excellent reputations, and received a mixture of rejections and acceptances. Bearing in mind the high cost at the schools who accepted me, the guidance counselor said, "How about a State University in New York"? I asked if any had a good journalism department, and he replied, "Well yes, the State University at New Paltz has an excellent Journalism Department." The tuition there was much more reasonable, and although I would still need to take out loans, it was doable.

Since the school was only two and a half hours from my home, and the price was right, I decided to apply. I sent in the application on a Tuesday and on Thursday I had my acceptance. My best friend Howie, who lived across the street from me and was also looking at schools, also applied and got accepted. This was great, as I would be going with my best friend, and being two years older than me, he already had his own car.

We arrived at school orientation, given our schedules, and assigned rooms in the dorm. The first issue is that I noticed that I was not assigned any journalism courses. When I questioned this, I was told that, not only does the school not have a journalism department, but they did not even offer a journalism class! So much for the expert advice from my guidance counselor, and I wanted to kill him. It was too late to transfer to another school, as the die had been cast. Besides, I did not handle change well in the first place. So be it, New Paltz it was.

I was lucky to be placed in one of the new dorms on campus, and they were all suites that had a communal area surrounded by four bedrooms. I didn't realize it at the time, but the system used for room assignments was the first letter of your last name, which meant that my friends throughout college all had last names beginning with either F or G. Nineteen sixty-eight was in the age of free love and peace, an age that I was eager to explore. I was totally free at the tender age of sixteen, and just walking around the campus exposed me to a world that was, for the most part, foreign to me. Long hair, drugs, drink, frisbees and blankets…this wasn't Kansas anymore, Toto. It really wasn't too hard learning how to fit in, as I kept telling myself to just go with the flow.

A month or two into the semester, I was lying in my bed late at night when I heard a commotion in the suite. There was laughing and excitement, but it was no big deal as I figured that drugs were at play. Suddenly one of my roommates barged in and told me that there was a girl here, and do I "want in." I asked him what the hell he was talking about, and he said, "you know, we are paying her." I asked him "paying for what"? The answer was, "you know, she's a prostitute, and you can go next." I told him that was crazy, and I would pass. The night moved on and our guest was moving from room to room. Meanwhile, I was getting a great deal of ridicule from the others, as I was the only one not partaking, and I eventually succumbed to peer pressure and took my turn. Yes, my virginity was lost to a prostitute, not exactly a romantic story of love at first sight. I felt horrible afterwards. Besides the fact that it was not enjoyable, I felt like a loser, as here I was in the land of free love, with limitless possibilities, and I paid money for it?

My younger age only became an issue regarding two things. If I asked out a girl, she would be two or three years older than me, and, if I told the truth about my age, that was sometimes problematic for the girl. Also, there were popular bars in town where students hung out, and the drinking age was eighteen, so being sixteen meant that I needed to secure some fake ID. We were all given school IDs, and they were credit card sized with raised lettering with your name and date of birth. I tried to manipulate the date of birth by applying heat to the numbers to make them soft, and then used a sharp object to mold the letters and change the date. However, it was a complete failure, and now my ID was a train wreck. I was then forced to try to sneak into the bars or try to distract the bouncer's attention. I was once on a date with a sophomore who was nineteen at the time. When my entry to the tavern was blocked, I was forced to come clean with my date, and from that point on she only wanted to be friends.

One of my first-year courses was a Spanish Language class, where the teacher was stunning, and she took my breath away. I told my friends about this teacher, and they asked why I didn't ask her out. I told them that doing so would be an absurd attempt, as there was no way she would agree, but they challenged me to do it and kept egging me on. After a few weeks I could not stand it anymore and decided to ask her on a date. I reasoned that she could not have been too many years out of college, so maybe she was twenty-four or twenty-five. This was so uncharacteristic for me, and I do not know where I got the courage, but I went up to her after class and popped the question. She looked at me and smiled. Time stood still. Did the smile mean that she was considering it? Or was it a look of "you sweet boy, I think not?" She thanked me but said that it would not be appropriate for a teacher to date a student. I wasn't completely crushed, as in my mind she meant that she would if she could.

My goal in college was to do as little work as possible, however, at the same time, I was proud of my academic career to this point and felt a need to keep up high grades. I decided to search out classes where the final grade was based upon a written paper. I knew that I could write well, so this gave me the luxury of coasting much of the year and simply bearing down near the end of the semester to research the papers that I was going to write. Of course, in the English department that became my major, that meant actually reading some books. I once did attempt to author a paper on a book I never read, but that didn't work out so well.

After writing my very first paper for my English professor, I eagerly anticipated receiving my grade for that submission. It turned out to be a C minus and I was shocked, as I had never received anything less than a B in anything in my entire school career. I was enraged and hurt because I honestly felt that the paper was solid. The professor held office hours off campus where students could make appointments to see him, and I scheduled an appointment, eagerly wanting to present my case and demand to hear a legitimate reason for my poor grade. His office was in a small old freestanding home, and I arrived about ten minutes early. The door was locked so I waited outside at the bottom of the steps, where I noticed a girl also waiting for the teacher's arrival. I started up a conversation, she asked why I was there, and I responded, "I am here to see that prick, Pohling." She looked at me and said "Ah, that prick is my husband!" Whoops. When Pohling arrived, his wife immediately went up to him to whisper in his ear, and it was then that I knew I was screwed.

I went into his office to sit down and hear his wrath. To my surprise he made no mention of me calling him a prick, however, the expression on his face and body language was anything but warm and fuzzy. He asked why I was there, and I answered that I wanted to discuss my poor grade. I stupidly remarked that I never received a C in my life, to which he replied "Well, you have one now and you deserve it." When I asked for specifics, he was vague, and instead simply said that it lacked coherence and needed work. I disagreed, but this was going to be a lost cause, as arguing would not serve any purpose at this point, and I still had a whole semester with him to get through. I worked hard in writing the second paper, and it was an A paper if I ever saw one. He reluctantly gave me a B, because giving an A to someone who called him a prick was out of the question. He was eventually forced to give me a final grade of B, and I licked my wounds and moved on.

To my surprise, the school added a journalism class, and I enrolled immediately. In one of our assignments, we were told to write an original parable, and as usual, I waited until the day before the paper was due. I was sitting around with my friends, stoned on my ass, and watching Star Trek on the TV in the common area. The episode, which old fans may remember, featured beings that were half black and half white. Boom, I had my idea, and scurried to my room to begin writing. This teacher would not hand you back your paper with a grade, as he was high tech, and instead gave the student a micro cassette that contained the teacher's comments and grade. There was only one problem, as very few in any could afford a micro cassette player, however, the school library had them available. I brought my cassette to the library, sat in a cubicle, and listened. "Mr. Ginsberg, I am giving you an A on this paper. However, the A is provisional because I recall something in the literature that was remarkably similar to what you wrote." That son of a bitch was watching Star Trek too! He simply did not want to admit it, or he legitimately could not recall the *classic* book that he read in the past. Either way, I had my A and was happy.

I started dating an attractive girl, and my friend Howie happened to be dating her sister. At their urging, we all decided to take a trip to New York City, as it was only a couple of hours away, and we could have fun. Howie had a car at school, and it was suggested by one of the girls that we share the driving. You could only get a learner's permit at age sixteen in New York, so that is the license I had, which meant that I was only eligible to drive outside of New York City, and with a fully licensed driver in the car. So, Howie and I devised a scheme to hide my age. I would drive until we were approaching the city limits, would then announce that I had something in my eye that was bothering me, pull over, and Howie would drive the rest of the way. That worked, but I found out later that the girls suspected that I was bullshitting. I am a lousy liar.

I recall that there was a buzz throughout campus. One of the major magazines came out with a story about colleges that had the most drug use, and our tiny little school ranked in the top ten in the nation. The school administration, along with all the parents, saw this as a black eye and damaging to the University. On the other hand, the student body saw this as a badge of honor, and celebrations commenced throughout campus. Academic excellence took a back seat to entertainment and partying, and I didn't see anything wrong in this hierarchy of priorities.

My roommate was a nice guy, but neurotic, and crazy to the point that he scared me. One night I jumped out of my skin at 3:00AM, as things were crashing in the room. I turned on the light and saw my roommate with a yardstick in his hand and moving the stick up and down the venetian blinds. I yelled "Stanley, what the fuck are you doing?" He didn't answer, and I quickly realized that he was still sleeping. I had a sleepwalker on my hands, and I figured that this was not an anomaly and could happen again. When I mentioned the incident to Stanley the next day, he had no knowledge of this occurring. Unfortunately, like clockwork, this happened every night around the same time, and it was frazzling my nerves and I needed to find a solution, but I had an idea. I went to the hardware store in town and bought a huge industrial sized pair of scissors. When it came time to go to bed that night, I grabbed the scissors and started to forcibly open and close them. "Stanley, do you know what I am doing?" He nervously said "no." "If you get up again tonight, I am going to cut your balls off with these scissors." He uttered an audible sigh and slight tremor. Sure enough, I heard the stirring at 3:00AM. I immediately reached for the scissors and began to open and close them. Stanley, still sleeping, let out a sigh of "ooooooh!" and did not arise. I repeated the procedure for a week straight, and Stanley never sleepwalked again. So much for traditional cognitive behavior therapy. I was a psychologist's worst nightmare, but it got the job done.

During my first year I befriended Marty, and the two of us were opposite in every way but respected each other and got along exceedingly well. He never smoked pot and weed had already become part of my life. Although Marty had short hair and did not do drugs (I had shoulder length hair, a beard, and smoked a ton of pot), the boy could drink. When you opened his closet there was a bar that rivaled the bar at the Four Seasons, with every kind of liquor along with all the tools of the bartending trade. I joined a fraternity that could have been the basis for movies, and the fraternity house was in an old building in town that used to be a mortuary. An orientation ceremony took place in the basement where they used to dress the bodies, which was a bit unsettling to a few of us, to say the least. Marty, on the other hand, joined the conservative and preppy fraternity on campus. The two fraternities could not be any more different, just like me and Marty. Marty had conservative political views, and my views were very liberal. I was Jewish, Marty was Catholic. Foul language was part of my vernacular, and Marty rarely cursed. I was interested in sports, but not so much for Marty.

Marty began inviting me to his home on holidays to spend time with his family. He lived in a sleepy, well-heeled community, which was only about an hour from campus. His family was huge, with many siblings, and one of Marty's sisters was born on the exact same day and year as me. They were a close family and very warm people who always made me feel welcome. During one visit Marty's mom asked him to pick up something from the village pharmacy, and I went along for the ride. When we entered the store, Marty bumped into one of his neighbors and Marty said hello and started to introduce me, "This is my good friend Bob…" and the woman extended her hand to shake mine. Then Marty continued and said "Ginsberg." As soon as the woman heard "Ginsberg" she retracted her hand forcibly and walked away. I was dumbfounded. Marty, "What the fuck just happened?" Marty laughed and said, "she probably thinks you have horns." This was the first time in my life that I experienced antisemitism, as I grew up in Brooklyn in a predominantly Jewish neighborhood. Brooklyn was a melting pot, and I had several good friends that practiced other religions, but prejudice was the furthest thing from our minds as kids.

One of my business idols to this day is Mike Nanno, an Italian born genial person in his fifties, who knew that about 10PM every night the campus was populated by students who were quite stoned and hungry. Like a knight in shining armor, Mike would go from dorm to doom in his shiny new Cadillac, which was filled with huge shopping bags that contained hero sandwiches. He would carry several bags into your dorm and make his announcement of the day's selections. "I gotta BLTs, I gotta tuna, I gotta ham and cheese, and I gotta roast beef." Our eyes would light up, as we were starving, and through our bloodshot eyes we saw this man as a Saint. Mike had the perfect business model, as he served a need, was appreciated, and made a nice buck.

In nineteen sixty-nine the Vietnam war was on everyone's mind, and the student body was politically active. I don't recall any student that believed that we should be there, and there were student demonstrations, takeovers of administration buildings, and organized protests. Most of the teachers joined in the protests, and not much serious schoolwork was getting done. The likelihood was that many of us would wind up going to fight in Vietnam, and the government held its first draft lottery that year, where people were assigned numbers based upon their birthday. If you were assigned a number of one to one hundred twenty-five, it was a given that you would be drafted. The drawing was televised, and students huddled around the common TV sets. The lottery was for kids that were nineteen or older, however, since I was still seventeen this lottery did not affect me, but I knew that if the lottery continued, my time would come. My roommate drew number one, and I saw the color drain from his face as he sat in stunned silence. I felt some empathy and compassion for Stanley, as I knew that this could put him over the edge.

Two happenings from the summer of that year have not faded from my memory. One was the first moon landing, as it was inconceivable and mind-blowing that man would walk on the surface of that magical orb suspended in space. I was visiting my parents at the bungalow colony when the event was taking place, and there was excitement about what we were about to witness. Few people had TVs, but there were a few, even though the reception was horrible and required "rabbit ear" antennas, plus one person to keep moving them around to find the best reception. Despite the fuzziness, we were all in awe of what we were able to see and hear. The future seemed limitless, and we were stunned as fantasy turned into reality before our eyes, a seemingly impossible accomplishment.

One month later I joined Marty (yes, Marty of all people) to go to Woodstock, and Marty and his friends from home rented a U-Haul van, which would be our home for several days. We piled into the van with anticipation and sat in traffic for what seemed an eternity. The New York State Thruway had to be shut down after becoming nothing more than a parking lot, and people were abandoning their cars on roads and began walking. One million people attempted to get there, and about five hundred thousand made it. We eventually arrived and found a place to park, but we were so far from the stage that we could only identify the band that was playing by the music. Woodstock was a fantasy world, a sea of people, blankets, smoke, drugs, and alcohol. What stood out from the experience was that everyone was sharing. Sharing their food, their drugs, their clothing, their bodies, or simply providing love, comfort, and reassurance to each other. There was no violence and no crime, and it was the only time in my life that I was in such an environment, and I doubt I will ever see it again, at least not in this lifetime. Meanwhile Marty, who had never partaken in any type of drugs, was convinced to take a small toke on a joint, and I have polaroid photos of him smiling, wearing a headband, and giving the peace sign. Years later Marty went on to become a successful attorney, with political aspirations, which troubled me because our politics were so different. I would call him every couple of years to remind him that I had Woodstock photos, and I would release them to the press if he ever decided to run on a Conservative ticket. Of course, I was kidding, but Marty never did run for office.

THE MESSMAN

I needed extra money and was looking for a summer job. My uncle was an executive for a company that made small home appliances, and he asked me if I wanted to work on a freighter. The people that worked in the factory all belonged to a union, which was inexplicably the Seafarers Union. I had no idea what factory work could have to do with the high seas, but I did not question it, as he knew people at the union and would get me hooked up. This required me to get a Merchant Marine license, which was required for working on large ships, but the minimum age requirement for such a license is sixteen, so I was good. After getting my license I was told to report to the Union Hall for assignment to a ship, which I did, and was assigned to a container ship that sailed from New Jersey to Puerto Rico. I was to be a messman, the lowest ranking person on the ship. Basically, I was a dishwasher, but my duties also included rising before everyone else in the morning and start prepping food.

I was not licensed to drive yet, so my dad drove me to the port in New Jersey. I grabbed my suitcase out of the car, said goodbye to dad, and sent him on his way. It took a while, but I found the gangway to the entrance of the ship, and I was met by a seafarer who told me how to find my quarters. This ship had been in dry dock for a year undergoing repairs, and this was its first voyage post repairs. I took one step into my cabin and was aghast, as the entire room was wallpapered with thousands of cockroaches. There was not an inch of metal that could be viewed. I don't believe in hell, but if I did this would be close to what I imagined. I picked up my suitcase, found my way back to the gangway, and told the sailor about my predicament. He laughed and said, "deal with it." I then said "Ginsberg, checking out" and walked off the ship. Yes, I needed the money, but not this bad.

Of course, I now had a predicament. Cell phones had not yet been invented and my father was on his way back to Brooklyn. I don't recall how I got back home, but I eventually did. I told my uncle about what happened, not knowing how he would react. However, he was not angry with me, but at his union contact for letting me be placed on that ship, and he made another phone call. I was told to report back to the Union Hall for reassignment, and I was assigned to another ship leaving from the same port, and once again got a ride from my dad. This ship turned out to be newer and I was relieved. My cabin was to be shared with two other guys, each a few years older than me. They were waiters, elite positions compared to a lowly messman. I was told to stow my stuff in the metal cabinet assigned to me, and that someone would come to wake me at 4AM. I did not have the same gear as the typical sailor, as I was convinced that, despite being only sixteen, I was losing my hair, and I had all sorts of creams and lotions in glass containers, remedies that I purchased from ads at the back of various magazines (or comics). In addition, I had pimple medicine and a variety of other toiletries and products.

I eventually fell asleep that night but was startled and awakened by large crashing sounds. The ship had set sail and all my unsecured items crashed to the floor and exploded. A brief time later I was visited by an imposing figure who was about six foot six, bald head, and all muscle, the perfect likeness to Mr. Clean and was there to escort me to the galley. I started to follow him, but after about five steps felt sick to my stomach, as the room was spinning, and I wanted to puke. Sea sickness had set in big time, and I was incapable of standing, let alone working. I pleaded with my cabin mate to take my shifts that day and promised to make it up to him, and I guess he had pity after seeing my green pallor, and he agreed. I spent the next twenty-four hours alternating between my bed and the bathroom. I made a few attempts to move around the ship but was the source of amusement for all the hardened seafarers. When I journeyed out to the rear of the ship, the poop deck, I asked one of the seafarers approximately how far offshore we were. When he replied about twenty miles, I wondered if I could jump ship and make it to shore alive. Fortunately, I didn't give it serious consideration, especially considering that I woke up the next day feeling fine and resumed my duties.

I came to enjoy sitting out on the poop deck in between my shifts, riding the huge wave crests and feeling the downward plunge. I began trying to engage some of the hardened sailors in conversation. They would work nine months straight, without a break, and would send most of their wages home to their families but see them rarely. They took two to three months off every year, left the ship with a boatload of cash, and lived it up with their family, and then the cycle started again.

When we reached port in Puerto Rico, the crew knew all the hotspots to frequent. I tagged along with all the crusty sailors, including the two younger waiters that were my bunkmates. The first stop was a dirty and disgusting strip joint, where the dancers looked like they were homeless, and most likely the last shower they took was in the prior month. One of the sailors yelled out to a dancer, "Hey, what do you got?" She grinned a toothless smile and said, "What do I got?" and then proceeded to pull down her panties, point, and yelled, "This is what I got!" I didn't know whether to laugh or cry. The crowd was enjoying themselves, but I just wanted to escape this madness. We hit a few more spots and stayed out most of the night drinking and returned to the ship about 3AM, where I slept for the hour until I got my 4AM wake up from Mr. Clean.

I made the journey back and forth for the rest of the summer, earned some nice money, and was grateful for the experience. I had lived a pretty insulated life to this point, but I learned some valuable lessons about being respectful of others, not judging people, and what hard work entailed.

COLLEGE LEARNING:
THE HARD WAY

I decided to move off campus my sophomore year and got together with friends to share an apartment in one of the village's garden apartment complexes. Many students did the same, and more than half of all the tenants were college students, a sort of dorm away from home. There were five of us in a two-bedroom apartment that had one bath, a good-sized living room, and an ample kitchen. None of us knew how to cook, but Howie made his best attempts and would often prepare meals. Money was an issue, but we all pooled a set amount every two weeks and made a shopping trip. Our purchases were mostly of the munchie variety, but Howie would insist on buying meats and other protein so we could maintain at least the semblance of a proper diet.

One of the guys came up with an idea for us to stretch our food dollars, as he discovered that we could apply for food stamps, because technically were a family of five, and none of us had any money in the bank. To apply we had to all drive to Kingston, New York, where there was a state office that administered the program. We found out that the combined household could not have more than $2,000 collectively in the bank, so we were all forewarned and brought our checkbook registers, and the interviewer did indeed ask to see our bank balances. I went first and showed that I had $342 in the bank. One by one we showed our registers, $240, $170, $425. That meant that so far, collectively we had assets of about $1,100, leaving $900 on the table. Then they got to my last roommate, and he showed his checkbook balance, $2,600, and if looks could kill, he would have died right there. When we got in the car we screamed, "Shmuck, what the fuck were you thinking?" but Paul could not lie and simply told the truth. As it turned out, the examiner had some pity on us and granted a small amount of money, funds we used to load up on extra Velveeta cheese and ice cream.

The apartment to our left was occupied by five female students, and three apartments to the right there was another group of four. We became very friendly with our neighbors, and that sometimes included certain privileges. On Thanksgiving we decided to invite them to a real Thanksgiving dinner, and Howie and I went to the market to buy a huge turkey and ingredients to make side dishes. Howie and I did the cooking, but I was really a mere assistant, and when it came time to take the turkey out of the oven, we looked at each other and asked, "What's that smell?" Nobody told us that you were supposed to take the bag and gizzards out of the turkey before cooking it, and it smelled so bad that nobody would eat, but everything turned out OK, as we got pizzas, wine, and smoked the night away.

There was a girl in the other apartment that I thought was the most beautiful person I ever saw, the kind of beauty that could take your breath away. She wasn't in any of my classes, but I saw her in the library once studying the same text that I had for my class. Still being quite shy when it came to meeting girls, I struggled with getting the courage to ask this goddess on a date. Part of my hesitancy was that I felt that she was out of my league and could surely have any boy she wanted, but I devised a plan, and I asked her if she would like to study together. She agreed, as she was having difficulty with the subject matter and invited me over to her apartment to hit the books. I could not discern whether this was a sincere desire on her part to improve her grades, or if she had some interest in me, but I cared not, and I dabbed on a little Old Spice cologne and headed over to her apartment at the appointed time. We sat next to each other on the couch and placed the texts on the coffee table. I could not concentrate, as she was even more beautiful up close, and we

36

kept talking and talking about all sorts of things, never looked at our books, and there appeared to be vibes that we were both feeling. Finally, no longer able to contain myself, I leaned over to kiss her, and she didn't pull away, a good sign. I then embraced her, moved my hands against her breasts, and she pulled away. Oh shit, I misread the whole situation. It was awkward after that, and we both opened our books, but shortly after I said goodnight, embarrassed and upset, and I didn't call her again because I assumed that she wanted no part of me. About six months later I bumped into a friend of mine who dated the same girl a year ago, and they remained friends. My friend asked why I never asked her out again, and I asked him how he knew about my experience. He then told me that she told him that she liked me very much but did not want to give the wrong impression by giving herself to me on the first date. In fact, she was terribly upset that I never asked her out again, thinking that I didn't like her. I was crushed, but it was too late now, as she had a steady boyfriend. The experience reinforced my belief that I didn't have a clue about understanding women, but it was a lesson learned.

Meanwhile I was getting almost all A's, doing very little work, and coasting. Since we were about a one-hour drive from Monticello Raceway, about once a week I convinced Howie to drive us there to play the horses. I would study the program and handicap the horses, always believing that I would hit it big. Some nights it was ten degrees outside, and I would wear a fur coat that my father made for me to help survive the harsh winters. Sometimes there would be less than one hundred people in the stands, and you could make a five-dollar bet and knock down the odds. Many of the drivers in harness racing at the time were known to fix races, but despite one driver's reputation, I bet on a horse being driven by him. As the horses were approaching the stretch run, I walked down to the finish line to watch the end of the race up close. My horse was in the lead, but as the driver was midway down the stretch, I saw him actively pulling back on the reins, slowing his horse down. He finished out of the money, and I was livid. Since the stands were empty, and since I was up close, the driver could hear me yell "hey, Sleepy Jim (his nickname), what the hell were you doing?" He heard me, turned towards me, and answered "Fuck You!" Yeah, harness racing was a classy sport.

Meanwhile, I continued to study the racing program every week, and there was one horse named Rusty Coast that I watched race several times, and he was a strong closer. He would be near the back of the pack but would always make a furious run down the stretch. He didn't always win, but almost always finished in the money (first, second or third). One week I noticed that he was racing and stacked up beautifully against the horses in the race, but there was only one problem, he was racing at Yonkers raceway, a two-hour drive away. However, this was my chance, and I could not let it pass me by. I started talking up this horse to all my friends, and five of us piled in the car to make our fortunes. I instructed everyone to be sure to bet the horse win, place, or show, guaranteed that they would cash, and when the race started our hearts were all beating fast with anticipation. We spent everything in our pockets, but all of us were already counting our winnings. As usual, Rusty Coast was nowhere to be found until he hit the stretch, as he started his run a little late, but I was not worried and calmed my friends. He started passing horses like the wind, but he was running out of room, as the finish line was fast approaching. He finished in a *photo finish* for third. That meant that the photo had to be examined to determine which horse finished third. The results were posted, our hearts sunk, and saying that I was not immensely popular at that moment is a huge understatement. We also made one major miscalculation, as we didn't have any money to pay the Thruway toll to get home. We checked under and behind the car seats, and combined with change found in our pockets, scraped together just enough. After this experience I gave up going to the track for the rest of my college career.

In my Junior year I moved to a nicer apartment complex, with predominantly the same crew of friends. Our school also had a reputation for spending the majority of its general funds on securing the top bands of the day, and concerts were held on the athletic fields, where half the crowds were not students at our university. Mid-year I developed a committed relationship with Ginny, who at the time was a pretty, conservative nice girl with few vices. We were together most nights, with her staying over in my apartment, or me staying in the trailer that she was renting. Unfortunately for Ginny, she began to pick up my vices, including recreational drugs. She was at my apartment one Saturday morning, and we were all excited about seeing Jefferson Airplane that night at the concert. Along with my roommates, we started the day with doing a "honey-slide," where we fried up marijuana in a pan, then mixed it with honey, and let it slide down our throats, a hearty breakfast. In the afternoon we all drank cheap Gallo wine, which came in gallon glass bottles, as quantity and affordability took precedence over quality. When the wine was all consumed, one of my apartment mates brought out some mescaline. Neither Ginny nor I had ever taken a hallucinogenic substance, and we were very apprehensive, but already significantly inebriated and decided to do it anyway. Nobody instructed us on the proper amount to take, and I found out much too late that we each took a triple dose.

I am not the personality that likes to lose control, as it makes me uncomfortable, and I was in for a rocky road. I saw what I interpreted as another universe, fractals and geometric shapes, colors that I had never seen before, and total disorientation. Meanwhile, I was scared for Ginny, as she seemed to want to jump out of her skin, and I was mortified when she ran out of the apartment and started sprinting in different directions. I thought that she would surely get into trouble, or be hit by a car, or worse, so I started running after her. I ran and ran, all afternoon, never catching her, at some point losing my shoes and running barefoot throughout the campus and village, the whole time freaking out that I lost Ginny. Evening came, and I somehow made it back to the apartment, where Howie was also tripping mightily, and the two of us engaged in conversations about what we were seeing. I eventually decided to go back out to resume my search, as it was now about 2AM, and I felt the same way I did that afternoon.

I found myself on the athletic fields. The concert had ended hours ago, and what I witnessed was a sea of trash, a vista of a vast wasteland, all in perfect silence. And then, off in the distance, I saw a man, dressed in white robes, and sporting an exceedingly long beard. The man had a garbage bag and was slowly and methodically picking up trash, and I distinctly remember blurting out, "Holy shit! it's Jesus Christ!" I stayed for quite a while just marveling at what I saw, an act of selfless benevolence, and then I eventually moved on to resume my search. Why a nice Jewish boy from Brooklyn would be seeing Jesus I cannot answer. I consider myself to be an open-minded skeptic, and to this day I cannot definitively say that I did not see Jesus. I made my way back to the apartment again but was worried that I would never come down from this alternative universe, and this would now be my life, but eventually the drug wore off and I looked at my bloodied feet, and around the bedroom. Howie's grandmother had given him an expensive Persian rug, which he put down in the bedroom. In our stupor we had evidently *day-glowed* the crap out of it, as it was now multicolored, unrecognizable, and ruined. Ginny turned up the next day and was safe, as it turned out that a friend spotted her running and took her home. That was the first and last time that I ever took a hallucinogenic substance.

As usual, I was looking for summer work to make money, and Howie had an uncle who was an executive in food services at the Concord Hotel. This hotel was the largest resort "in the borscht belt," and featured fifteen hundred guest rooms, a dining room that seated three thousand, and had amenities that sprawled across two thousand acres. It was a veritable city within itself, a hideaway in the mountains, and we secured jobs as waiters. Howie had experience working there before, so he was a captain in the dining room. We worked mostly for tips, but the job included room and board, and I was happy to be employed. The only way to describe the hovel in which we stayed would be a rustic crack house, as it was dark, dingy, musty, and falling apart. I hated such accommodations but was not overly concerned, as we rarely slept. I had four jobs, a waiter for breakfast in the coffee shop, a waiter for lunch on the patio, a waiter for dinner in the dining room, and an usher in the night club. Being a waiter in such an environment is demanding work, and I had much trepidation before carrying those large trays with eight meals on them. All meals, in unlimited quantities, were included in the fee that the guest paid, a server's nightmare, as food was the major attraction, and guests would just keep ordering to get their "money's worth." During my first day I dropped a full tray as I was attempting to put it down, spilling a drink and meal on a guest. I was mortified but managed to escape being fired.

Working the lunch shift made me the most nervous, as the head chef was a miserable human being with a bad temper, and he would bark orders and disparage the wait staff constantly. One meal I delivered was a steak to a guest who ordered it medium, and when the guest took a bite, he became furious that it was not done enough and ordered me to take it back, which meant that I had to face Mussolini. The chef glared at me and said, "Really, not done enough?" He then proceeded to throw the steak on the floor, step on it a few times, and put it back on the plate. "Here, bring it back to the shmuck who ordered it. See if he likes it now." It was futile to protest, as this chef, for reasons beyond me, was a fixture at the resort, and I was not going to change him or his disgusting antics. Inexplicably, the diner thought that the revised steak was now suitable, something that made me contemplate the power of thought. What also made me sick to my stomach was watching how the tuna and egg salad was delivered, as the monster sized portions were made in another kitchen and delivered to our kitchen in huge bus trays, but these trays were the same trays used to collect dirty dishes. They were not cleaned, or lined, and I wonder how many people fell ill. After the summer was over, it was a long time before I began eating in restaurants again.

Meanwhile, my relationship with Ginny was becoming serious, and I brought her home to meet my parents. Although they would have preferred it if she were Jewish vs. Irish Catholic, to their credit they gave her a warm reception and treated her well. Ginny also brought me home to meet her parents. For those old enough to get the reference, the only way that I can describe that experience is, her father was Archie Bunker, and I was Meathead. The man was an Archie clone, same views, same politics, same prejudice, and a marked disgust for people of the Jewish faith. Thankfully, he pretended that I did not exist for most of my visit, and I appreciated the limited interaction and respite from my unease, as I couldn't really breathe again until the visit was over, and we left the premises. Our relationship broke apart in my senior year, when Ginny told me that she had another boyfriend it came totally unexpected, and I was crushed. However, when I look back upon this today, it was the best thing that could have happened, as our relationship was based more on lust and convenience than love. A marriage to her would surely have ended in divorce, and I never would have met my true love.

In nineteen seventy-one I was nineteen and a senior, and three of us rented an old farmhouse that was about five miles from the village. The owner of the farm lived off the main road, and to get to our house we had to turn into his driveway and make our way a mile down a rocky curvy road and navigate a rickety bridge. The farmhouse was more than a century old and had apparently never seen any type of improvement since it was built. There was a make-shift shower with trickling water and some ancient appliances, but there were three bedrooms, one for each of us. The total rent was $100 per month, and we used to argue each month over who would be $33.34 cents vs. the other two who paid $33.33.

It was as private as you could get, which we appreciated. However, we were cautioned by the farmer that he allowed his friends to hunt on the grounds, and on more than one occasion we heard shots coming too close to comfort. On the other hand, during tomato harvest he would bring us buckets full of the best tomatoes that we had ever eaten, a veritable feast. There was one major downside to these living arrangements. The farmer had a firm rule about no women being allowed in the home while we were tenants. This made bringing home dates and girlfriends somewhat problematic, but not impossible. We first tried asking our companions to slouch down in the front or back seat while passing the farmer's house, but he was shrewd and caught on to this ruse. The solution was simple, however, as we simply had to ask our dates to get into the trunk for the short but bumpy trip. Amazingly, we had few if any objections to these requests, and our missions were successful. However, there were a few close calls where the farmer made a surprise visit, but we were inventive in hiding our contraband.

Now nineteen I was eligible for the draft lottery, where my number was drawn, and it was seventy-two. Numbers up to one hundred and twenty were sure to be drafted, so I knew that shortly after I graduated, I would get the notice. I managed to graduate "Cum Laude" and received my B.A. in English, and after graduation I returned to my parents' home to figure out the next step. What the hell do you do with an English degree? I had no desire to teach, so I went out into the work force. My first job was selling dresses in the garment district of New York City, where I was a total failure and soon searched for another job. I had a brief stint leasing and selling office trailers that were used on construction sites as temporary office space. I loved my boss, but this was boring and certainly not a career, and I moved on to selling exercise equipment, a job I also secured through a connection of my uncle, and that job lasted a few years. I used to sell the equipment to retailers and wholesalers, and my time was split between the office and the road. One perk was that I got to travel to trade shows with the executives. The owner of the company was flashy and had expensive tastes, and we ate in some of the finest restaurants where the meals were exquisite.

I received my notice from the draft board to appear for a physical at Fort Hamilton army base in Brooklyn. I had a bad knee, as I tore up cartilage twice, once playing basketball when I was fifteen, and then again playing football at seventeen. Orthopedics was not very advanced then, and each time I was injured they placed my knee (which was blown up to twice the size) in a full leg cast for six to eight weeks. They would remove the cast after the allotted time had passed, but the knee remained damaged. I was told that I should bring my x-rays to the draft physical, and I did.

I remembered all the stories that my older friends told me about their draft physical experiences, as this was during a time that kids were doing crazy shit to avoid being drafted. Many of my older college friends were now getting their physicals at the same time as me, as they were exempt while they were still in school, and we graduated together. My neurotic roommate from college read somewhere that severe hemorrhoids would keep you out, and for three months prior to his physical he wiped his ass with the coarsest sandpaper available. It worked, as the examiner took one look inside his rear, gasped, and sent him packing. Getting out for psychological reasons was also an option. Another friend, when required to give a urine specimen, picked up his container of urine, looked the examiner in the eye, and drank the contents of the container as he smiled. That didn't work. The best story I heard was from my friend, Eric. While at the army base you would go from station to station carrying your original records, and in the middle of the process he simply walked out a door, with his records, and never looked back. He was never contacted again.

During my draft process, we were all told to enter a closed room for our hearing tests. There were about twenty sets of headphones, and we were told to press a button every time we heard a tone. For the entire time, every guy in that room would either keep pushing the button non-stop, or not press it once, but nobody failed the hearing test.

Part of the procedure was that everyone had to take a written test. I still had that innate desire to excel in tests, so I decided to just do my best. Besides, if I tried to fake it, who would believe me? After looking at the test I realized that eighty percent of the questions had to do with geometric reasoning, mechanics, and spatial relationships. I sucked at this, as my brain simply did not work that way. The passing grade on the test was sixty-five, and when they announced the test results, I got a sixty-six. I was aghast. High school dropouts surrounded me, and they got scores in the nineties, showing me that education had little to do with intelligence, at least for this test.

When I told the examiners that I had x-rays for a doctor to look at, they said that I had to see a specialist in the afternoon, as they had agreements with private sector orthopedists that would come in during certain hours. Since I had a couple of hours to kill, I decided to use that time to run around the army base. The day before the physical I was also running for most of the day on Jones Beach, and at the end of my run around the base, my knee was significantly swollen, and I was noticeably limping. I showed up for my appointment with the orthopedist and presented him with my x-rays and a written report from my own doctor. He took one look at the x-ray and said "sorry, but you can't be drafted with this knee." I replied, "don't you even want to look at my knee?" He replied, "get out of here." And so, I did.

AND THEN WE MET

I was hanging out at Jones Beach one Saturday and I happened to bump into my college friend Eric. Spotting him was unlikely, as the beach on a summer Saturday was packed with thousands of patrons. We started talking and he said, "Hey Bob, I am going out with this girl tonight, and she has a cute sister. Want to come?" I had never been set up on a blind date before, but hell, I wasn't doing anything, so I agreed. He gave me the address and the girl's first name, and I planned to meet him there. Her home was in the Westchester suburb of Mount Vernon, about an hour's drive from Brooklyn.

Although I had already graduated from the college environment, I was still smoking pot every day, mostly at night. However, this was a special occasion and I needed to mellow out, so I smoked a joint in the car while traveling to my date. Ah, the stupid decisions we made when we were young. I arrived at the home about fifteen minutes early, and I was stoned on my ass and very happy. I rang the doorbell, and the dad opened the door with a smile. I said, "Hi, I'm Bob." I then proceeded to give him a hug and kiss him on the lips. Really. He was understandably confused and dumbfounded, but not upset, and much later told me that he thought that I was just a very friendly guy. I could also see that he was wondering who the hell I was, and why I was there, and I told him that I was there to see Frances. Meanwhile, Frances walked out from the other room, and asked who I was. I had naturally assumed that Eric would have told her sister that I was coming, but the idiot did not.

This was not love at first sight. In fact, she was not pleased at all to be put in this position, was angry, and wanted no part of me.

Meanwhile, Eric strolled in and announced, "This is my friend Bob. I invited him to come along so that we could double date." The only reason that Frances, after negotiation, agreed to go was that we were going to her favorite place, Rye Playland. On the way there I was told that her name was Phran, with a PH, and I remarked that it was an unusual spelling. Phran was not much in the mood for talking, still upset, but told me the reason behind her name. As a young child her family lived on a block that had a drug store nearby. She was just able to read and examined the sign that said Pharmacy, and it was then that she, the rebel that she was, decided that her name would henceforth be Phran, as if they could spell Pharmacy with a PH, so could she.

We made it through the date and there was no kiss goodbye. I asked if I could call her again and she said that she wasn't sure. I left for home, but this time I was determined not to make the same mistake I made in college, and I was going to be persistent. This girl was extremely attractive, bright, and somewhat mysterious. She was going to Brandeis University in Boston on a full scholarship, so I didn't have much time to wear her down before she left to go back to school.

She finally agreed to see me again. I again drove to Mount Vernon, although not stoned this time, and I had a pleasant conversation with her parents. Phran and I went out to dinner, and during conversation Phran told me that both of her parents were concentration camp survivors. Their families were virtually wiped off the face of the earth, but they survived. Her parents would never talk about that period to Phran, or her siblings, as they wanted to shield them from the horror. We had a nice dinner, although I still suspected that Phran was not really into me, and at the end of the evening, again there was no kiss, as I wasn't sure what her reaction would be, so it was safer not to push it.

I think it was the third or fourth date that I brought her to Brooklyn, we went out to a seafood restaurant in Sheepshead Bay, and I was wearing a blue velour sport jacket, trying to look respectable for this special date. I loved lobster, and this was the place to get one, but I quickly found out that Phran had never eaten lobster, as she grew up in a kosher home, so that was out of the question. However, for some reason, perhaps the wine, she decided to join me in ordering a lobster, and when the two large lobsters were brought to the table, I saw that Phran did not have a clue as to how to eat this thing. I assured her not to worry, as I was a professional and would assist. I grabbed one of her claws and told her that I would crack it open for her, exposing the meat, and I gave the claw a mighty crunch with my nutcracker. Lobster juice exploded all over my velour jacket, face, and hair, and that might have been the first smile that I saw from her. Actually, it was more of a huge laugh. My jacket was ruined, but she found it amusing. Perhaps she was warming up to me?

Phran returned to Boston, but I had exercise equipment clients in the area, so I could detour to spend time with her in college, if she agreed. By this time, I think she liked me, but I wasn't sure. I arranged to visit an account on a Friday and asked Phran if I could spend the weekend with her in her dorm. She agreed, and although we had been seemingly enjoying each other's company, I still worried that his might backfire. I arrived at her dorm room, knocked on the door, was told by her roommate that Phran was out, and I started talking with her roommate for what seemed like hours. Phran eventually walked in, and I was a bit miffed that she knew I was going to be there but chose to make me wait. There were only two beds in the room, one for her roommate and one for Phran, and it was obvious that I would be sharing Phran's bed. I remember that the room TV was on, but the lights were off. Phran's roommate was wearing a see-through negligee, and she kept walking back and forth in front of the TV, providing me with a show, and I wondered if she knew what she was doing. It turned out that she did, and Phran could only smile.

As I write this, I am trying to remember the first time that Phran and I had sex, but I am ashamed to tell you that I don't recall. It could have been while her parents were out in Mount Vernon, or during one of her Brooklyn visits to my parents' home, or at

Brandeis. I do recall, regardless of where, it felt right. There was no doubt in my mind that I would marry this girl, and I knew it from the start, and I proposed to her in nineteen seventy-three, less than a year after we met. My mother gave me her mother's engagement ring, so I was all set. I bought one of those giant teddy bears, and then proceeded to write about seven different clues which I strategically placed around my home in Brooklyn. The last clue brought her to the ring hidden in the Teddy Bear, and at least she acted surprised. We married in nineteen seventy-four, when Phran was twenty and I was twenty-two.

We went to Aruba for our honeymoon, and neither of us had ever been out of the country, and we were excited. We soon realized that the only people who went to Aruba in June were honeymooners, as we met six other couples and all of them got married on the same day as us. We started hanging out together at the resort, drinking, gambling, swimming and more. I decided to try parasailing and watched attentively as the staff fit me into a harness, and I was a bit apprehensive as the boat took off and I soared into the sky attached to a rope. The views were great, and I was incredibly happy, until the landing. As it turned out, the instructors were not very attentive or skilled at bringing people back to the beach, and instead of a nice soft beach landing, they crashed me into a tall palm tree. I wasn't seriously hurt, just angry and embarrassed, and that ended my parasailing career.

One night all fourteen of us went out to dinner at a local upscale restaurant. It was the kind of restaurant where they bring out your meal in covered trays and the waiters uncover all the meals at the same time once everyone has been served. After dinner, when it was time for dessert, the waiter asked for our choices, and one person in our group asked the waiter if he knew where we could score some pot. That was a bold move, as you never know who you were talking to, and I had visions of being led away in handcuffs by the local police. The waiter did not reply to our query and returned to the kitchen, which made me even more nervous. He returned a few minutes later with a giant covered tray, which he placed in the center of the long table. He uncovered the dessert, and there before us were fourteen perfectly rolled giant joints. We laughed, tipped him generously, and returned to the resort to party. As it turned out, pot was plentiful at the resort as well, all one had to do was ask any staff member. When it was time to return home, there was no way that I was going to get on a plane carrying grass, so I buried the leftovers at the bottom of a palm tree. I wonder if anyone ever dug up the buried treasure during the last forty-eight years.

After returning home we rented an apartment in Brooklyn, after borrowing money from a relative for our security deposit. It was a small second floor apartment in a detached two-family home. We were both working but had only one car, and Phran would take the bus and the subway to commute to New York City every day. Once per week she would stop on the way home at a fish store near the subway stop and bring home a bunch of steamers. We loved them, they were cheap and easy to prepare, and an extravagance to which we looked forward. Meanwhile, I decided to try my hand at gardening, growing marijuana plants to be specific. After all, how hard could it be? I read a bit about the subject, went to the store to buy small pots and soil, and separated the seeds from my personal stash of grass. I started six plants, and because they needed an abundance of sunlight, I lined the plants on our windowsill facing the street. I watched and nurtured them each day and envisioned the moment when I could begin harvesting my home-grown treasure. It turned out, however, that my green thumb was more of a black thumb.

My landlord lived on the first floor and was often gone for long periods of time. One day Phran and I returned home from shopping, and as we approached our house, we saw two police cars. As it turned out, my landlord's alarm system was blaring, and the police officers were walking the perimeter of the home looking for any forced entry. I started to panic. What if they glanced up on saw my window garden? We decided to simply wait in our car until they left, which they did after about ten minutes. When we walked back into our apartment, we both laughed at our fear of being caught. The plants were so anemic looking that even a horticulturist would have trouble recognizing the plants as being marijuana. Shortly thereafter I ended my gardening career and trashed my crops.

We needed a headboard for our bed, but money was too tight for that expense. As usual, Phran had a workaround, and she told me to buy an inexpensive piece of plywood that was the same width as our bed. After I managed to secure this, she set about wrapping the board in a colorful fabric, and the board was to be hung on the wall over the bed. While she was out for a meeting, I was given the task of hanging her masterpiece, and I told her not to worry, as I had an idea of how to do this. To say that I was not handy is a gross understatement, as the only tools I ever held were a hammer and screwdriver, and even with those I was lost. However, I did not want to disappoint my love, so I had to complete this task. First, I tried to hang it like a picture, but soon realized that it was too heavy to hang in that fashion, but then came an epiphany. I went into the kitchen cabinets and unscrewed all the hooks that supported the hanging teacups, and I figured that I needed about fifteen hooks for the job. I would simply screw them into the wall in a straight line, and then place the bottom of the board in the hooks. Brilliant idea I thought, and I was enormously proud of myself, that is until I placed the board. The openings in the hooks were not wide enough, the hooks were not level, and after I managed to get the board supported on the bottom, the top tilted out about six inches. Phran came home, looked at my project, and simply said "What the fuck did you do?" She did not know whether to laugh or cry, and in the subsequent forty-six years of marriage, she never again asked me to do a home project.

We decided to host our first dinner party and invited Howie and his new girlfriend to join us. We got a few bottles of wine, Phran cooked a meal, and we were excited at the prospect of being real grown-ups. Howie arrived and introduced us to his new love, whose name now escapes me. She was attractive, with long brown hair and a bubbly personality. A little too exuberant and happy to my taste, as I am more of a glass half empty guy. We all shared a bottle of wine and some cheese, engaged in some pleasant conversation, and moved to our kitchen table for dinner. The table was a small glass and chrome square, all we could afford at the time. I was sitting opposite Howie's date, and midway through the meal I felt a leg brush up against mine. My first thought was that it was Phran, but I quickly realized that she was not the source, and I dismissed this as an accident due to the lack of leg space. But then a foot started moving up and down my leg, seductively. I glanced across the table and saw a slight smile, and it was then that I knew I had a problem. How was I to handle this situation? If I did nothing, I would run the risk of Phran noticing and thinking that I was encouraging my aggressor. On the other hand, Howie, who was a huge person and could have kicked my ass, might feel the same way. I considered simply moving my chair back a bit to be out of her reach, but that would surely seem suspicious. Instead, I decided to announce that I was getting up to retrieve some soft drinks from the refrigerator and stood up. Surely, if this girl had any sense, she would move her leg away. Instead, after standing up I stumbled back into my chair. Her foot was caught in the bottom of my bell bottom jeans (yes, I still was wearing these).

It was then painfully obvious to all what had happened. Phran, who I later found out was watching the whole episode from the start, simply said to the girl "You do realize that this is a glass table?" Howie, on the other hand, turned beet red with anger. He announced that the evening was over, and abruptly stormed out of our apartment with my paramour trailing sheepishly behind. Phran was not angry with me and was somewhat amused, however she did mention that I could have ended the situation sooner. Howie came over the following day, not to kick my ass, but to apologize to me and Phran. He ended his relationship with his girlfriend that night.

In her spare time Phran started selling Tupperware to make extra money. She was successful at anything she tried and was recruiting other people to sell as well. Every time you recruited another person your name was entered in a raffle, with the prize being a new car, and something inside her told her that she would be winning the car. It was one of her *knowing* feelings, and not based on reason, evidence, or performance. One evening she went to a Tupperware meeting, and I was getting a bit concerned that it was well after 11PM and she still wasn't home. I had gone to bed but couldn't sleep, and I then heard noise coming from the stairwell that led up to our apartment. I shot out of bed, completely naked, and opened the door to the staircase to greet Phran. Before me, standing there in all my nakedness, stood about seven Tupperware ladies who came to celebrate Phran winning the car. I was embarrassed, but they thought it was hilarious, and I hoped that it wasn't a reflection upon my manliness. The car that she won was a Ford Pinto, and that was around the same time those cars were recalled for exploding gas tanks. We never even took possession of the car, as we sold it back to the dealership, and the two thousand dollars was a great deal of money to us and helped pay bills and splurge a little at the same time.

After a year in the apartment, Phran announced that I *had* to get her out of Brooklyn, and it was more of an ultimatum than a request, as she hated the environment and wanted to move to either Long Island or Westchester. We drove out to Long Island one day, looked at ten houses, and narrowed it down to three. We put bids in on all three houses and decided that whichever owner accepted our bid was the house we would buy. One owner did accept the same day, and we signed the contract. It was a large three-bedroom home, with a possible fourth bedroom downstairs off a great room. It was seven times the size of our apartment, and we spent every dime we had on the down payment. By this time, I had started in the insurance business, and I was confident that there was a great deal of upside with regards to money, so we rolled the dice. Luckily, we started to be more comfortable financially, plus I was always one to spend more than one would consider to be prudent.

Building an insurance agency from scratch was stressful, and I often wondered if I was on the right track. I was not a salesperson by nature, and handling rejection was difficult to process. Selling insurance was purely a numbers game. Cold calling names from a purchased list, or simply out of the phone book, was a daunting task that I found distasteful and somewhat demeaning. However, the formula was simple, as calling one hundred people meant getting about five to ten "leads" which would result in a couple of sales. Going door to door soliciting business owners was not much better, and I grew weary of a process that was mostly ineffective. I decided to use my advertising skills to be smarter in getting business and engaged in various direct mail and display advertising campaigns. My agency started to grow, and I became motivated and intrigued by being able to use my creative side instead of the monotonous previous protocols. I was able to overcome my meager sales skills by utilizing passive marketing, eventually resulting in a successful and profitable business for forty years.

Vacations were out of the question in the early years of home ownership, as our focus was simply on being able to pay the mortgage and utilities every month. Our friends Joe, Linda, Lenny, and Val asked us if we would like to join them for a weekend at a campground in upstate New York. When I heard the word campground I shuddered, as if there is anything that I am not, it's a camper. In my entire adult life, other than post surgeries, I cannot recall one day that I did not take a shower and wash my hair. I flunked out of Boy Scouts because they could not teach me how to tie a knot, and my survival skills were non-existent. However, my friends mentioned that there were cabins that we could rent for the weekend, and a cabin in the woods sounded like something interesting that I could handle. We set out on the trip with all sorts of paraphernalia, including bedding and blankets.

When we finally arrived it was late, and we were exhausted from the drive. Off in the distance we spotted the cabin and set out to enter our palace, unwind, and have a drink. When we entered the cabin, we were all shocked, and not in a good way, as dirty and disgusting were adjectives that did no justice to these environs. The smell was atrocious, the windows would not open, and there was evidence of a previous fire. Joe, Lenny and Phran wanted to stay and lit a fire in the fireplace to warm up, but after the cabin filled with smoke and a window mysteriously slammed shut, Linda and I announced that we were out of there and started to repack the car. Off we went, now late at night, in search of a motel. We had no maps, and GPS existed only in one's imagination. After what seemed like an endless journey on back roads, we finally made it to a main highway, and surely, we would see a motel sign off in the distance somewhere. But I had another problem, as I desperately needed to take a shit. As I write this, I realize how ridiculous that expression is, even though it was part of the Brooklyn vernacular. I was not taking anything, as I only wanted to give. I had to go so badly that my eyes were bulging as I squirmed in my seat, and I started praying to the bowel gods to make a motel appear. Meanwhile, to my dismay, Phran and my friends all thought my dilemma to be humorous.

Finally, in a vision from heaven, I spotted an elevated motel sign in the distance, and I hoped that I could make it. And then it happened, as Joe's car started chugging and sputtering, and Joe announced that we had run out of gas. I started screaming and called my best friend every derogatory name that I could come up with. How could he let this happen, and didn't he realize the seriousness of the situation? After about a minute of this, everyone in the car started laughing hysterically. The running out of gas was a planned joke and it worked to perfection, and Joe was very lucky that I did not own or carry a weapon. We made it to the motel and luckily, they had three vacant rooms. I was the first to grab the keys, run to the room, and try to release my pain. It was a rundown motel, but at that moment it was a five-star hotel to me. In a cruel twist of fate, I was holding it so long that I couldn't go!

Decades later, Phran and I once had a private audience with a world renown Swami from India. One of his messages to us, through a translator, was "When you need to go.....go." I didn't understand it at the time, but when I heard this, I remembered my cabin experience and recognized the truth.

Pregnancy Roller Coaster

Not long after we were married, we decided to have children. I love children, and I much prefer the company of children to most adults. Babies fascinate me, as it is the only time in our life when interactions and emotions are pure and unfiltered, and when a baby laughs it is the most beautiful sound imaginable. I am also fascinated by toddlers, especially the way you can see their minds work as you try to anticipate their next move. I am not sure why I love children so much, but perhaps it is a longing to see innocence and light amidst a world often dominated by darkness.

We tried and tried for many years but had no luck and decided that it was time to see a fertility specialist. Phran went through batteries of tests, and with each new physician I gave sperm specimens. At one specialist, before arriving I was instructed to bring the sperm sample with me, but it was winter, and I was cautioned to be sure to keep the sperm warm. Well, that's all I needed to hear. I warmed up our car with the heater on, put the sample in my armpit, and then put on my fur coat. The doctor's office called me later that day to tell me that my sperm had zero motility. After I told them about my precautions the nurse said "well, you cooked the damn things!" I brought in another sample, and it was fine, and it was determined that Phran needed to undergo a surgical procedure to correct a situation that was contributing to her infertility. She healed well, we were back in the saddle, and Phran had to keep charts to determine the optimal times of ovulation. The windows of opportunity were exceedingly small, and I would get calls from her ordering me to get home immediately, as it was time. Not very romantic, but we were on a mission.

Meanwhile, Phran was started on a fertility drug, and it was the same drug that you often read about because it sometimes resulted in people having multiple fetuses or resulted in birth defects. We tried unsuccessfully for another year, with regular doctor visits in Manhattan. One day Phran got the call...we were pregnant! We were ecstatic that we were finally going to have a child, and we went about our normal schedules, all while trying to contain our exuberance. About six to eight weeks later Phran started feeling terrible cramps. She made it to the bathroom, and she realized that she was having a miscarriage. The doctor later did whatever he had to do, and told us to keep trying, and assured us that we would get pregnant again. She did get pregnant again and we were cautiously optimistic, however, at about the same time duration into the pregnancy, she miscarried again. This went on for a total of five miscarriages and we were depressed, exhausted, and started to discuss adoption for the first time.

The doctors determined that, although Phran could now get pregnant easily, her body was not producing enough of the hormone HCG (Human Chorionic Gonadotropin) to sustain the pregnancy. She did get pregnant again, but this time the doctor ordered complete bed rest, twenty-four hours a day, except for going to the bathroom. They taught me how to administer HCG injections, which I gave to her regularly. I served her all meals in bed, and thankfully my mother and friends assisted in helping to take care of her. As we were approaching the six-to-eight-week point, we were both on edge. There was a cautious sigh of relief when we made it to ten weeks. At fifteen weeks we allowed ourselves to breathe a bit, and apprehension started to turn into excitement, however, with the possible repercussions of taking the fertility drug, we could never truly relax during the whole pregnancy. Her belly was getting bigger with every day, and we were getting close, and our excitement was hard to contain. Because her pregnancy was such high risk, all her doctors and hospital were in New York City, which was about a ninety-minute drive away, without traffic. The day finally came that Phran went into labor. We had her bag prepared, and we rushed to our car to begin the journey. It was during the afternoon rush hour, and the Long Island Expressway was a parking lot. I was climbing out of my skin with anxiety due to the traffic, but Phran kept reassuring me that everything would be OK. When I finally reached the toll booth at the tunnel, I screamed at the cop and told him that my wife was in labor, that I needed to get her to Lenox Hill Hospital, and asked if I could get a police escort. He told me that I would get there quicker on my own, and I should do what I had to do to get there. I was passing red lights, racing when there was open road, and honking my horn.

We finally made it to the hospital after what seemed like an eternity. I left the car out front, which you don't do in Manhattan, and ushered Phran into emergency. Her doctor had already been alerted, and Phran was brought upstairs to maternity. Her obstetrician examined Phran and told us that she was still hours away. Shit, so much for racing there like a maniac. I went back downstairs to move my car, which luckily was still there, and quickly went back to maternity. We waited, and waited, and waited. After about eight hours the doctor took me outside the room to fill me in on what was happening. He had administered Pitocin to induce labor because he felt that the baby would soon be in distress, and he wanted to avoid a C-section if possible. Phran and I had taken Lamaze classes to prepare for this, and I was her coach. While I was outside the room talking to the doctor, we both heard "Coach, where the fuck are you!" The doctor and I both looked at each other and he said, "I think it's time to get in there."

I held Phran's hand, kept wiping her forehead with a cool cloth, and felt helpless as she writhed in pain as epithets spewed from her mouth. Finally, the doctor announced that it was time and said it was OK to push. I watch in awe, but still very much aware of the risks we took. I saw the head make its way out, and it looked good. Then the arms, then hands, at which time I counted every finger. Two legs, two feet, ten toes. I was in a stupor, amazed, and happy beyond belief as the baby was born. Then Phran said "What is it, boy or girl?" I said, "how do you tell?" I can't explain it, but I was so focused on it being a healthy baby that its sex was immaterial. The doctor just looked at me and said "Really?' That shook me back to reality and I checked. "Oh, it's a boy!"

Jonathan was a happy and healthy baby, and we knew that we wanted another one. Phran got pregnant fifteen months later, and this time it was determined that she had to stay in bed for only the first half of the pregnancy. She went into labor almost a month early, so we were concerned, and once again we had to make that journey into Manhattan.

When Kori was born, she looked OK, but the staff quickly whisked her away and we could not hold her, as Kori was rushed to neonatal care. We were told that she had hyaline membrane disease, and although she was only three- and one-half weeks premature, her lungs were not yet fully developed. The chief neonatal physician explained to me that this was the same thing that the Kennedy baby had, and that baby did not survive. However, he reassured me that technology had now advanced to the point that they now had respirators and equipment that could be used with tiny premature babies. The prognosis was guarded, and he said that Kori had a fifty/fifty chance of surviving. She was put into an induced coma and was hooked up to what seemed like a hundred different tubes and wires, all while on a respirator. Parents were allowed in the neonatal unit, and that space became our home. She was born at almost five pounds, but they wanted her weight to drop to ease the strain on the lungs. Weeks went by, but we were told that she was hanging in there. One night I was there alone, and a thought occurred to me that there were always twelve to thirteen babies in the unit, and there was rarely a boy present. I thought that to be odd, and I approached the doctor and told him of my observation and offered my explanation that the boys were somehow stronger. He looked at me and said, "No, you have it all wrong. The boys never make it to this point." This stayed with me my whole life, as I learned a lesson that day about which was the stronger sex.

We both stopped staying with Kori round the clock and one of us would go home to sleep. I remember heading home alone one late night, and silently praying to God that Kori would survive. I was not religious, and only prayed when it was mandatory in a religious service, but I was pulling out all stops. I made a lot of promises that night, some of which I did not keep. To this day I wonder if those unfulfilled promises affected the course of my life. After a month in the neonatal unit, Phran and I arrived early one morning, and we were told that this would be the day when they would try to remove Kori from her respirator. We were also told previously that they had no idea of knowing how oxygen deprived she was, and for how long, which meant that there could be either brain or eyesight issues. We were told to get a cup of coffee and come back in an hour, and when we did return, we saw that the curtains on the windows to the unit were drawn. I peeked in and saw all the doctors and nurses standing over Kori. The blood drained from my body, as I realized that they had started the procedure, and something went wrong. However, when one of the nurses spotted us, she came running over and told us not to worry. They had not removed the respirator yet, but there was a malfunction in the equipment and false alarms started going off. Shortly after, they did remove her from the respirator, which seemed to go well as she was thankfully breathing on her own. Now we just had to wait as they did tests to determine if there were any lasting effects.

Kori had suffered no permanent damage, and the time finally came to bring her home. Even though she was our second child, we watched over her constantly. After she was home about a month, she developed pneumonia and we frantically called our pediatrician, who told us to take her to a hospital close by, and he would meet us there. This hospital had a horrible reputation, nothing like the hospital that saved Kori's life, but it was the closest to us, so we had no choice. Kori was admitted to the baby ward, and our pediatrician gave specific instructions to the nursing staff. They had to give her medicine through an IV, but after a month of tubes and IVs stuck everywhere in her body, they could not find a viable vein. It was decided to put the IV in her head, something that appalled us, but it was explained that it is often done this way in such cases. They would not let us stay in the unit, so Phran and I returned home to try to sleep. When we arrived early the next morning and saw Kori, we were horrified, as her head was blown up twice the size. They had missed a vein and fluid was filling up her head. After screaming at the head nurse, I made an emergency call to our pediatrician, "You better get the fuck down here NOW – they are killing my daughter!" He arrived about an hour later, took one look at Kori, started blasting the staff and the doctor on duty, and they immediately removed the IV.

I don't recall how they got the medicine into her, but they used a different protocol. Phran now insisted that we be allowed to stay with Kori at night, and, after hearing Phran and looking at her body language, there was no way that they were going to refuse the request. During the night I noticed that the bright lights always stayed on, and I asked one of the nurses if they ever dimmed the lights, and her answer was "No sir, if we did that your baby be dead and we wouldn't know it." Phran and I looked at each other and said, "Check please, we are out of here." Unfortunately, there was nowhere to go until Kori got better, and we were forced to let her remain there for a few days. Fortunately, she responded well to the medications, and we were able to take her home after a short stay.

SUPER CARS AND CASTLES

We were invited to attend a fundraiser for the charity that our good friends help run. Major sponsors of the event donated raffle prizes, and the tickets were available for purchase before the event. The tickets were one hundred dollars each, which was pricey thirty years ago, but I think we bought at least three tickets before we arrived. At the event, the organizers had more raffle tickets available for purchase, and these tickets were lined up on a display table. Phran grabbed my arm, brought me to the table, pointed to one ticket and insisted that I buy that specific ticket. I protested, pointing out that we already had three tickets. She then told me that she just had a vision and saw the two of us standing on the stage receiving the first prize, which were two first class airline tickets to Germany, donated by Lufthansa.

Phran always had a keen sense of the way things would play out, and I always attributed this to her superior intellect, logical mind, and reasoning skills. However, there was something more, as she sometimes tapped into sources of information that were non-physical in nature. In any event, one didn't say no to Phran, and I bought the ticket to which she pointed. About fifteen minutes later, that ticket number was called, and there we were on stage as an executive from Lufthansa presented us with the tickets, which were replicated on one of those huge placards.

When we got home, we were wondering what we should do. Germany, considering that her parents were in concentration camps and their families lost, was about the last place we wanted to go. However, we could not let our prize go unused, so I called American

Express Travel, and booked a trip called "Super cars and castles." The trip was a first-class endeavor, and we were treated well. We were greeted at the airport by an executive of Lufthansa, escorted to the executive lounge, and eventually accompanied to our seats on the plane. The gourmet food and pampering impressed Phran, and I could tell that she was excited. We landed in Frankfurt, and an Amex representative greeted us at the airport with the vehicle we had chosen. We had the option of either a Mercedes convertible, a BMW, or a Porsche, and I chose the convertible. We were handed the keys and given maps (this was long before GPS was invented) and embarked on our journey. We were to stay in a different medieval castle every night throughout Germany, Switzerland, Austria, and Lichtenstein.

It was raining, and there we were on the Autobahn, where there was no speed limit on most of the road. I was doing one hundred and fifty miles per hour, and I noticed a car behind me in my rearview mirror, and he was on my tail with his turn signal on. I had read that in Germany people don't flash their brights when they want to pass you, they use their turn signal instead. I said to Phran, "Do you believe this guy? I am doing a hundred and fifty and he wants to pass me? No way!" She insisted that I switch lanes, and I eventually complied. I did not travel at that speed for long, as I quickly realized that your attention and reflexes must be razor sharp at that velocity.

Phran was an excellent map reader and navigator, and we made it to our first destination, Castle Weitenburg, without incident. It was a castle in Germany that was built in twelfth century. Typically, the present owners of these castles would retrofit a few rooms to rent out, as keeping a castle running is extremely expensive to say the least. We were served a magnificent meal in the dining room and there were no other guests that day in the castle.

We made our way back to our room and marveled at the thirty-foot-high ceiling and carved ornate mahogany four post bed that looked to be original. It was raining and thundering and lightening kept illuminating the room, a perfect atmosphere given our surroundings, which Phran found to be a bit spooky. As we lay in the immense bed watching the storm, we could not stop thinking about who had slept in this very bed over the last nine hundred years. Phran and I discussed writing a story about people like us who visited a castle and "mystically" took on the bodies of the original residents. If we only knew that in later years, as our lives changed, we would be taking such subjects seriously! I also thought about the wars and sieges that took place over the centuries and wondered how many times the castle had changed hands. It was a surreal experience, mystical and sacred, and I knew that we were lucky to be there.

While staying at a castle in Switzerland, we took a day trip to Mount Pilatus, a massive peak that overlooked Lucerne at an elevation of seven thousand feet. There were cable cars that would take you to the top of the mountain, which sounded like fun. We boarded the cable car and the first thing that I noticed were other passengers, on this warm summer day, wearing jackets and winter garb. I wanted to laugh at their folly. When we reached the peak and exited our cable car, I immediately realized how smart the others were, and how foolish I was. My teeth were chattering from the extreme cold at this elevation. Fortunately, there was a souvenir shop, evidently put there for idiots like me, and we proceeded to buy an assortment of sweatshirts and jackets.

While still in Germany we decided to visit Dachau, one of the most notorious concentration camps. We felt obligated to do so, as if it was paying homage to Phran's family. The villages on the road to Dachau were beautiful and peaceful, a stark contrast to what we were about to witness. As we entered the road to the concentration camp site, it became very eerie as the skies darkened and opened to a massive downpour that flooded the streets and parking lot. Some of the original structures in the camp were left standing, including several barracks, the showers where people were gassed to death, and the crematorium where they were burned. There was also a small museum on site that was lined with huge photos of the atrocities and contained many artifacts and history lessons. I wondered how the current Germans reacted to seeing this and was glad that such evidence still existed and could not be ignored, a reminder that nothing like this should ever be allowed to happen again. As we walked through the camp and the barracks the hairs on my arms were standing up, as the energy was tangible, and when we walked by the gas chambers I wanted to vomit. Unspeakable evil took place, cruelness that was beyond comprehension, and I shuddered at the thought that this could happen again.

We continued our castle expedition, and we approached Castle Steinberg in Wurzberg that you could see from miles away. It was perched on top of a mountain and was a very impressive sight. You made your way to the castle by driving on a narrow road that kept circling the castle as you rose higher. The problem was that there was literally one foot of space left on both sides of the car, with no guard rails, no place to turn around, and we were a few thousand feet high. I kept driving, slowly and carefully, but we never saw any entrance to the castle. It's not a Holiday Inn with a neon sign, and we had no way of knowing where the entrance was. We were approaching the end of the road, and I had a sinking feeling as I realized that we missed the entrance, and I would have to back down the treacherous road. Phran started yelling that we were going to fall off the mountain and die, and I should not attempt to back down. I told her that we had no choice at this point, and she needed to trust me. Phran now took up residence under the dashboard, refusing to look. I would not let on as I was reassuring her, but I was scared shitless at what I was about to do, and I started my winding backwards descent as slowly as possible, constantly reassuring Phran along the way. After about fifteen minutes I saw what looked like an entrance point and entered a gate, and being a bit frazzled I hardly noticed the intricate details of this magnificent structure. Thankfully, alcohol was abundant in the castle dining room, and Phran was able to calm her nerves with a large glass of red wine, even though she was still pissed at me for putting our lives in peril.

After dinner I mentioned to Phran that there had to be a dungeon, and it likely still had suits of armor and torture apparatus.

There was nobody around and I wanted to check it out, and, since Phran was an adventurer, it didn't take much convincing, and we quietly started to make our way down a winding stone staircase. The problem was, there were no lights to guide the way, so we kept one hand on the wall. We kept going down and down, in an endless circular pattern, and after about ten minutes we reached the bottom. The anticipation of what we were about to see was killing me. I kept running my hand along the wall hoping that there was a light switch, and there was one. I flipped on the light, and there in all its glory was a German bowling lane. Nothing else, just a few bare tables. I was so disappointed, but we made the best of it by bowling

Castle after castle, adventures through the past, and the trip was memorable beyond words. As I reflect, I realize that there were no cell phones, which meant no convenient cameras. I don't think we took many pictures, if any, and it was a lesson in simply experiencing the now. Today, the masses seem consumed with capturing moments of time in a photo, usually as evidence that they were there so they could show their friends. You can get aggravated trying to capture the perfect sunset instead of marveling at the beauty, often missing out on the joy of simply experiencing. The castle experience was wonderful, and we capped the trip off with visits to London and Paris.

ALICE'S STORY

Since I have already told you about Phran's parents being concentration camp survivors, I must tell you about the day her mother told me how she escaped death at the hand of the Nazis. First, you may have noticed that I attributed this story as coming from Alice, but Phran's mom's name was really Barbara. Phran and her siblings often called her by her first name, which was the source of admonishment, as she vehemently would answer by telling them that it is not right to call your mother by her first name. Phran, always having a reply for everything and having a wicked sense of humor, told her that she was right. From that point on they would all call her Alice, which she eventually accepted for some reason, and that became her permanent name as far as her children were concerned. I might add that this was around the time that Alice Crimmins dominated the news, a woman who murdered her own children, but I digress.

Over the years I became very close with my in-laws, and they treated me like their own son. One day, when Phran was elsewhere, Barbara told me this story, after asking me if I wanted to know how she survived the camps. Phran's mother and father were from the same town in Hungary/Czechoslovakia, but her dad was about twelve years older. Phran's dad, Zoltan, was very much in love with Barbara, but she was only sixteen. Zoltan wanted to marry Barbara, but she said "Zoli, I would not marry you even if you were the last man on Earth!" Then Hitler came to pillage their town, and just before they arrived Zoli took the family jewelry and buried it in the ground near his home. Everyone was put on trains and taken to various concentration camps, and the village razed.

After being a prisoner in the camp for a while, Barbara was herded into an empty warehouse building, where it was well known in the camp that, if you were put there, you would be sent to the gas chamber the next day. Dawn came and Barbara knew that this was her last day on this Earth. She happened to walk all the way to the rear of this building and noticed a door that presumably led outside. She turned the door handle, and to her great surprise it was unlocked. She knew that if she opened the door, she would most likely be shot to death instantly, but what the hell, she was going to die that day anyway. She summoned enough courage to open the door, and immediately saw a line of prisoners on their knees as guards walked the line taking a head count. She knew that her only chance was to join the line, but nobody seemed willing to take the chance of making room for her. She then noticed a woman about fifteen feet away motioning her to come over. The woman made a bit of room, and Barbara fell to her knees as she joined the line.

However, Barbara knew that she would have a problem when the guards counted one more person than there should be. The guard was about to reach her, when suddenly sirens started blaring across the camp. There was some disturbance elsewhere in the camp, everyone in line was ordered to immediately return to the barracks, and Barbara followed the crowd. Later that day, everyone that was in the warehouse building was gassed to death. About three days later the Allies arrived at the camp and the prisoners were liberated.

Meanwhile, off in the distance, stood a frail Zoltan. Barbara told me that at that point, Zoli was the last man on Earth, and she knew that it was "B-Shert," a Yiddish term that means "meant to be." In other words, her soulmate. She agreed to marry Zoli, who managed to make his way back to where his home used to be and dug up the jewelry that he buried. Two wedding rings, which had been in the family for several generations, were later given to me and Phran by Zoli and Barbara to be used as our wedding bands. We were so honored to have that family history become part of us. We treasured the rings and I hope to pass them on to another generation. Barbara had an uncle who was a Captain in the U.S. army, who found Barbara and Zoli and helped them get settled in the U.S.

This story had a significant impact on not only me and Phran, but on our children. It taught me how the slightest decisions we make reverberate throughout the universe. If Barbara had never noticed and had the courage to walk out that door, Phran would never have existed, as well as my children, and right down the line. Yes, it is a story about courage, but also a reminder of the worst that humankind has to offer, and how far we have strayed from the reasons that we were put on this Earth.

Bailey was profoundly affected when she heard Barbara's story, and it became the subject of many essays that she had to write for school, as the affront to humankind during the Holocaust not only scared her but saddened her deeply. She was inspired by her grandmother's bravery and escape, but at the same time was troubled by conversations that she sometimes had with Barbara. She would often hear Barbara talking about people from other countries or faiths in a derogatory fashion, and she could not reconcile this with Barbara's experience. In her essays she commented that she could not fathom how anyone that experienced such atrocities at the hand of others, savageness based on race or ethnicity, could pass judgment on others. It was inconceivable to her that one could retain any prejudice after experiencing such an atrocity.

THE NEXT MOVE

We stayed in our first home in Long Island for ten years, and it was time to move. By now I was doing well in my insurance business, and we could stretch our wings a bit. There was an area on the Long Island Sound that Phran had scouted, and she really wanted to move there. We looked at a few homes in that area, but they were so far out of our budget that we postponed that dream. Instead, we moved into a nice suburban community, where the homes were large, and each had at least an acre of land. We found an interesting home that we could afford, and after some negotiation bought it, did some remodeling, put in a pool, and made it our own. There were plenty of children in the neighborhood and that pleased us. Phran and I decided that two children were enough, and not wanting to press our luck was the main reason. That is until we went out to dinner one night with my colleague and good friend Hubie and his wife. Over dinner we drank too much and Phran drove home, where I collapsed in bed very drunk and even more amorous. That night is when our third child, a beautiful girl we named Bailey was conceived, and when I found out Phran was pregnant I called Hubie and blamed it on him. Phran did not have to stay in bed while pregnant with Bailey, and everything went smoothly. Still the same doctors and hospital, but there was less caution.

Raising three small children, each two years apart, was a bit difficult, as I was working every day, and Phran got involved in politics. She approached politics with the same fervor and dedication as all her other causes and interests. She was all-in. Our time demands were extremely challenging, and we decided to get full time live-in help. We went through quite a few people, and we had to get rid of them all at some point. We discovered that one had a drinking problem, one would give the baby homemade remedies without our knowledge, and another could not manage the tasks at hand. Bailey, being the youngest, spent a lot of time with one of our helpers. When she started to talk, her first word was "mama," but soon after, unexpectedly one night, she said "Jesus Christ, Lord have mercy!" Phran and I looked at each other dumfounded.

We finally hit upon a great housekeeper, Stacia, and she became part of the family for many years. Because Stacia could be trusted implicitly, it gave Phran and I the opportunity to take quick breaks or mini vacations. We had a tradition, as every year Phran and I would take a weekend and check into one of New York City's best hotels and treat ourselves to a Broadway show and fine restaurants. It was our escape. One time we checked into a large suite at the Drake hotel, an upscale hotel that no longer exists, and our suite was spacious, with numerous alcoves and doors. I will preface what I am about to say by telling you that I have a horrible sense of direction, as you can take me around the block, and I will have difficulty finding my way home. As far as I am concerned, GPS was the best invention in the last one hundred years. Phran, on the other hand, was a self-named human compass, as you could take her anywhere once and she would never forget. She loved maps, although she rarely needed them, and was my navigator by car or foot wherever we went. So here we were on a Friday night, we had just come back from a fabulous dinner during which we shared a bottle of wine, after cocktails. We came back to the room, and we had about an hour before we had to leave again for a late show. I lied down on the bed and smoked a joint (yes, my college habits persisted). Phran and I made love, and I then announced that I was getting up to take a shower. I opened the bathroom door and stepped in, the door slamming shut behind me. Except it wasn't the bathroom. There I stood, naked in the hallway of the Drake Hotel, as the elderly couple in the suite next to us exited their room. With a sheepish smile I covered my privates with my hands and said, "Hi." They gave me a look of disgust as I frantically began knocking on the door for Phran to let me back in. She did, called me an idiot, but roared with laughter. You may have noticed by now that there appears to be a theme of me finding myself in awkward situations while naked. If you only knew the half of it.

Phran never felt comfortable in our new neighborhood, and she referred to many of the women she met as "Stepford Wives," as if their husbands bought them jewelry, they were happy. Most homes had fancy cars parked in the driveway, but sparse cheap furniture in their homes, as it was all about outward appearance. At one point, Phran joined a tennis group that would meet and play once a week. There was a jewelry boutique at the tennis club, and her fellow players would buy jewelry in between sets, which Phran found hard to believe.

We had a large pool, and some parents would simply drop their kids off at our house, expecting Phran to watch them. There was a time when a male doctor in the neighborhood dropped his son off, and when Phran questioned him why he thought it was OK to drop off his son and leave, his reply was that it was the duty of the women in the neighborhood to watch over the children. That was the wrong answer, and I am sure that Phran came awfully close to cutting his dick off after berating him.

Phran had excellent parenting skills and was a great mother. However, as it was in my own family growing up, it turned out that Phran was the disciplinarian in our household, while I remained the good guy, and this became the source of countless arguments between us. I would always try to mitigate the punishments, or occasionally argue on behalf of our children in the matter. One time Bailey did something wrong, had her privileges taken away, and was in deep trouble with Phran. Bailey was hiding out in the boiler room, not wanting to be near her mother, and I remember walking down there and saying to Bailey, "Bails, this is so bad that even I can't help you out of this one."

Our children are all very smart but have different personalities and strengths. Jon is intelligent, stoic, and has a logical mind and great business sense. Kori is gifted intellectually, and even went to a special school for the gifted for a while, where she did just enough to get by without doing any work. Bailey was equally bright, but outgoing, contemplative, funny and adventurous. We never had any issues with our kids regarding behavior in school with Jon and Bailey. Kori, on the other hand, was quite another story.

Do you have any idea what it is like to receive a call from the principal of your child's school letting you know that your daughter brought a vibrator in for "Show and Tell?" It is not a call you want to get. Before you jump to conclusions, here is the back story. About five years after we moved into our home, I decided that it was time to go down to the storage room and continue to unpack boxes, and Kori came down to join me as I was sifting through a box. I pulled out a contraption that I didn't recognize. It wasn't a typical vibrator, as it was a round disc, but when I saw a protrusion and noticed that it vibrated, I realized what it was. Many years ago, Phran got it as a gift from one of her friends, and it was never used. Kori asked me what it was, and I had to think quickly. This was around the time that Star Wars came out and was wildly popular, and I told Kori that it was a voice disguiser. She asked me what that was, and I held the vibrator to my throat, turned it on, and started talking like Darth Vader. Kori thought that this was very cool, and I then put it back in the box and we went upstairs. Unknown to us, Kori snuck down to the basement at night, found the vibrator, and put it in her backpack. She demonstrated in front of her class the next day, to the horror of her teacher.

That incident was the first of many for this child, and we were on a first name basis with the school principal. A little while after the first incident, Kori struck again, and I received another call from her teacher advising me that my daughter brought in a pair of her friend's panties for "show and tell." Kori had a sleepover at her friend's house the night before and was searching for another unique item. This time the school meant business, and Phran and I were summoned to a meeting with the teacher, principal, and school psychologist. The teacher presented the account of what had transpired, told us about the panties, and included the fact that "they weren't particularly clean." The psychologist stepped in. "Mr. Ginsberg, what do you plan on doing about this situation?" I thought about my reply, but all I could come up with was, "I don't know about you, but I am going home to lock my underwear drawer!" I saw a slight smile from the principal but looks of malice from the other two, as evidently that was not the answer they wanted to hear. If looks could kill, I would be dead from the stare of the psychologist. The principal stepped in to slightly lessen the tension, but we knew we needed to have a long talk with Kori, once again.

I tend to have a good relationship with everyone, so despite some annoying personalities among the men in the neighborhood, I never had any problems. I started a weekly poker game and invited a diverse crowd. Poker nights included much gossip, bragging, bravado, and laughs, but at the same time it was serious business because of the stakes. The game expanded to two nights a week but getting out a second night was not easy for me, so I stuck to one. We would occasionally go out to dinner with some of the guys and their spouses, but we were busy, and it wasn't a regular thing. I was also an active tennis player and joined two organized leagues, where I suspect that my opponents tended to underestimate me once they saw my heavy knee brace, and that worked to my advantage. I also decided to become a coach of Jon's Little League team, something that I enjoyed immensely but was very time-consuming. During my coaching career I realized that I was not treating my own son fairly. I was very much conscious of not appearing to favor my own son in my decisions, so he would often bear the brunt of my own insecurities, usually in the form of not getting the playing time he deserved. This experience served me well in later years, as I came to realize that ego often interferes with rational decisions that should be based upon evidence.

My favorite activity was people watching, and there was certainly a cast of characters to choose from among my neighbors. Directly across the road from me was Dhruv, a medical doctor from India who moved to the United States about seven years prior. The next closest home to Dhruv was owned by Steven, a member of our card game, and saying that Steven and Dhruv did not get along is a great understatement. One day I came home from work early and decided to relax in our screened in patio. My home was in a valley, and we looked up at the homes of my neighbors. I glanced up from reading the newspaper and saw Steven walking on his front lawn. He seemed distressed and I didn't know why, but something told me to watch the scene unfold. I saw Steven march across his lawn towards Dhruv's home at a rapid pace. He knocked on the door and Dhruv emerged.

Steven (screaming): "Your dog just shit on my lawn!"
Dhruv: "My dog did not shit on your lawn!"
Steven: "I just watched him do it. There is still steam coming off it!"
Dhruv: "Ok, you show me the shit!"

Now it is starting to get interesting, and the two of them storm off together towards the excrement in question.

Steven (pointing) "There! That is what your dog did!"
Dhruv: "Look, I know my dog, and I know my dog's shit. That is not his shit!"

Dhruv then turned around, went back to his home, and slammed the door. I then watched Steven go into his garage, retrieve a shovel, and scoop up the poop. He then paced to Dhruv's house, flung the crap at the front door, and returned home satisfied that he got revenge. Yes, these were two grown men, both well-educated and successful, who exhibited tribal behavior. I enjoyed the play immensely, especially the part where the medical doctor was able to identify his dog's excrement. That was an impressive and bold claim.

Our family really enjoyed our pool, especially the night swimming. I would heat the pool to ninety degrees, turn on all the pool lights, and the kids would have endless fun and competitions off the diving board. After the kids went to sleep Phran and I would go skinny dipping, that is until the day that Dhruv and his wife Yvette invited me to their home. I looked out their kitchen window and noticed that, because of their elevation, they had a direct view into our pool. I remarked to Yvette that she had a beautiful view, to which she replied "Yes, nice ass Bob!" I can't say that it totally stopped my night swimming, but I was a bit self-conscious from that point on.

During our ten years in that home, I started to realize that I would go through periods of depression. Not depression in a clinical sense, but a general feeling of hopelessness that had no apparent root cause. Outwardly I had all the trappings of a content life, nice home, nice cars, a growing business, a beautiful family, and all the toys I wanted. However, there was a persistent feeling of dread and recognition that there was something missing. In my adolescent and teen years, I was also convinced that I would live a short life, and as I now reflect upon my life, I am open to the possibility that all these feelings were the result of perceiving the future. My uneasiness and periods of depression could have been the result of an inner knowing that Bailey's death would devastate my life. Also, it is possible that it was not my own early death that I foresaw, but that of my daughter and those around me.

Phran became heavily involved in school politics after she uncovered corruption that was taking place. There were protests, campaigns, legal battles, and trips to the State Capital for meetings, and her life became consumed by her mission to make things better. However, after several years it became apparent that Phran's activism was becoming a real problem for the Superintendent, and the teachers who supported him retaliated by taking it out on our children. That is where we drew the line, and it was painfully obvious that we needed to move.

Phran began to once again look in the north shore hamlet that she loved before we settled in our present home. Home prices were now much higher, so finding a suitable home that we could afford was going to be a challenge, even though our income had increased over the years. Over the previous fifteen years Phran always kept an eye on the marketplace, and she looked at fifty houses in the area during over the years. She now spotted a huge home that had been up for sale a while and asked me to go look at it with her. I saw the price and almost choked, as I hate looking at things that I cannot afford because I am an impulse buyer. If I saw something that interested me, I wanted to act upon it, so I saw it as futile to investigate things that were beyond our means. Since I refused to go, Phran took Bailey with her to see this home. As the two of them approached the home, they saw that the grounds were completely overgrown, and it was hard to find the entrance. Once in the home they were awestruck, as the home seemed to go on forever. There was little furniture in the house, so it was obvious that nobody was living there for quite a while. When Phran and Bailey made it up to the second floor, Bailey started laughing at what she thought was the master bedroom and marveled at its sheer size. When they discovered the actual master bedroom, they both could not believe their eyes, as the room was immense, the size of most apartments, and they could not wait to continue exploring the rest of the seven thousand square feet and basement that awaited them. Outside, most of the two plus acres were wooded, a plus for those like us that treasured our privacy.

They both came home all excited and pleaded with me to put in a bid. I told them that it was out of the question, as it was beyond our means, and the real estate taxes alone exceeded forty thousand dollars. Phran was not giving up and counseled that you never know what will happen until you try. She was wearing me down, and I told her that if I put in an offer, it would be embarrassing to me, but, of course, she told me to suck it up and at least try. I put in an offer at a number that was our absolute limit, a price that I was sure the real estate broker would find ridiculous. When she heard my offer she said, "Oh my," but let us know that by law she had to present the offer to the sellers. The sellers apparently said a lot worse, and the dream was dead, especially because I had already advised the broker that I could not entertain any counteroffer made by sellers. About a month later, the broker called and asked us to raise our offer, as the home was still for sale. I raised my offer a bit, it was submitted, and again soundly rejected by the sellers. Phran and Bailey were extremely disappointed, but we moved on, or so we thought. Six months later the broker called once again and advised that we were not supposed to know this, but the sellers were engaged in a bitter divorce. The husband was extremely bitter, and because he did not want the house sold, he had rejected every offer that came in. His wife's attorney petitioned the court, and a judge ruled that henceforth he must accept the third offer to which he was presented. Since the ruling was made, he had rejected two offers, so if we made another offer now, it had to be accepted. I was asked to come up a bit in price, just to ensure that the offer was deemed to be somewhere in the ballpark. I did, the offer was accepted, and we went into contract.

Meanwhile, the home was caught up in a "War of the Roses" scenario. Walls were damaged, glass broken, and even though it was a newer home it was in a general state of disrepair. As is customary, we had a home inspection done and presented the seller's attorney with a list of items that needed to be addressed, at a cost of forty thousand dollars. The day of the closing finally arrived, but neither of the two sellers appeared. Their attorney started the closing by announcing that his clients declared bankruptcy that morning, and they would not be making any of the repairs. He then looked at our real estate broker and told her that she would not be paid her commission, and this might have been the only closing in history where the broker started to cry. We felt terrible for her, as this would have been a large commission. Phran and I decided that we would forget about the money for the repairs, as we knew we were getting a deal on the home. Four hours of negotiations ensued among the brokers, lawyers, title company and bank, and it was finally determined that we could close, and the broker would settle for fifty percent of her commission.

We were finally handed the keys, drove immediately to our new home, and walked in to find that the temperature in the house was over ninety degrees. We soon realized that while we were at the closing, the previous owner was in the home stealing everything that could be detached, including all the thermostats, alarm and stereo systems, fixtures, and anything that he could carry. We had done a walk-through before the closing and all was well, and since he would be the only one with access, we knew he was the culprit. Not only was he enraged about having to sell, but irate about the selling price. We took it all in stride and gradually embarked upon various repairs and new projects that would make this our true home.

The home was in a secluded hamlet that had a reputation as being a wealthy neighborhood, so Phran and I were concerned that it could be like the one from which we just escaped. We were pleasantly surprised that, although there were certainly wealthy families, everyone seemed down to earth and far from ostentatious, and the kids made a bunch of friends and settled into their new schools easily. There were no businesses of any type allowed in our village, and since the nearest store was twenty minutes away, we had to plan our trips accordingly. I was commuting one hour each way to my office, but every evening I was treated to a different sunset as I made my way over the causeway that connected our hamlet to the mainland, and that made the trip worth the trouble. I was a bit worried about how our kids would fit in when invited to the homes of their friends. Our family was anything but formal around the dinner table. I tried to explain to our children that normal families sometimes dine in clothing other than sweatpants and burping and farting were usually frowned upon. As it turned out, my fears were unfounded (at least to my knowledge) and controversy was avoided.

My deal with Phran was that she would give up politics if we moved there, so for the first time in her life she was without a specific cause to champion. Instead, she focused on managing the home, which was by no means an easy project. We had little interaction with neighbors, and I would describe our life there as being in the witness protection program. Of course, we met some adults that were the parents of our children's friends, but there was little or no socializing. The houses were distanced apart, and in the summer, you would not even know that neighbors existed. There were no sidewalks in the community, and we didn't even have a doorbell (yes, the previous owner ripped that out too, and we never bothered to replace it). We did, however, install a heavy dragonfly door knocker. Deliveries were sometimes problematic, as if you were at the other end of the house, you often did not hear the knock.

Although Phran was often deadly serious and focused, she had a wicked sense of humor and loved to laugh, and usually the frivolity was at my expense. It could be something simple, like waiting for me to weigh myself on the bathroom scale, and quietly sneaking up behind me and putting her foot on the back of the scale. She would wait for me to wail that I had gained ten pounds, and then laugh hysterically. However, sometimes her plans were more subtle, quite elaborate, and required great patience. We had a national wildlife preserve about two hundred yards from our home. It was originally the site of an old Gold Coast mansion during the gilded age in the late eighteen hundreds and early nineteen hundreds. The mansion was long since tore down, but the heirs to the estate donated the land to the government. There were several walking trails, and we used to take walks through the preserve in all four seasons. During one walk in the Spring, I happened to notice an attractive and colorful bird resting on a branch just above us. I was struck by its beauty, but I knew absolutely nothing about birds. So, since Phran knew something about everything, I asked her the type to which I was pointing. She immediately replied that it was a "double cocked summer warbler," which was rare in our area.

About a month or two later, I had a potential new client in my office, and we were making small talk as we got to know each other. I asked about his hobbies and learned that he was an ornithologist who had traveled the world identifying rare species of birds. I remembered our walk, realized that this was my time to score some points, and I mentioned that I too had recently spotted a rare species of bird. His ears perked up as he asked me to which type of bird I was referring. I proudly told him that it was a double cocked summer warbler. He looked at me with disdain and indignantly said, "There is no such bird, sir." At that moment I realized that Phran got me. As soon as I got home that evening, I started to tell Phran what happened, and she simply smiled. You would think that the *double cocked* would have tipped me off to her ruse, but I am a trusting idiot.

TRAVEL

W e did not travel that often, but when we did, we made it count. On one trip we went to a little-known island in the Grenadines called Petit St. Vincent. To get there, we had to take a commercial flight to Barbados, and once there we were greeted by a representative of the resort who led us to a two-passenger plane, where we would fly to the island of Union. That was a bit unsettling, as I could swear that I saw our pilot just get out of a taxi that he was driving, but I could not be sure. Once we landed in Union, we were directed to a boat that was owned by the resort, and when the vessel docked in Petit St. Vincent the owners of the island greeted us, with drinks in hand for us to imbibe. Those old enough to remember the TV series Fantasy Island can relate, as it must have been modeled after this island.

The island then consisted of about fifteen different luxury cottages, each with a different placement on the island. Some were on the beach, and a few were on cliffs overlooking the beach and ocean. When booking we selected one of the cliff residences, completely private, and the views were as astounding as described. For meals, one could choose to go to the pavilion to dine or eat in your cottage. The menus were wonderful, and in the morning, you could watch the staff coming out of the ocean with the fish entrees that would be served that day. Outside each residence were little poles with two flags. If you put the red flag up, the staff knew that you wanted privacy and would stay away. However, if you wanted anything at all, at any time, you put up the green flag, and patrolling staff in carts would take your order and bring you what you wanted.

The flags were put on the beach too, so we decided to test it out to order two margaritas. I put up the green flag and a couple of minutes later staff asked us what we desired, and five minutes after that our drinks were in hand, and I remember telling Phran that I could get used to this.

At the time there was no phone service, no internet, and no TV, and you were going to relax whether you liked it or not. All the guests kept to themselves, but there were occasional beach barbecues where one could mingle if they so desired. It dawned on us that nobody would ever know that we were there, and we wanted to document our stay. We brought a camcorder with us, and we decided that we would both go down to the beach and film us from our cottage deck on the cliff. We didn't have a tripod, but we figured out a way to balance the camcorder on a table at the correct angle facing a specific spot on the beach. We turned on the camcorder and rushed down the winding path to the beach, where we then faced the camera and started waving like idiots. Later that evening we decided to eat in the pavilion, and we met another couple. They approached us and let us know that they saw us waving to them from the beach. They had the other cliff residence and just thought that we were very friendly.

On another trip to the West Coast and then Maui, we discovered something interesting. We traveled with our cousins, Ducky and Shorty (yes, everyone in my family had nicknames). Since they loved fine dining as much as us, we ate in some great restaurants, and Phran was keeping a diary of everything of note that happened during the trip. One restaurant was particularly good, and everyone tasted the sauce in one of the dishes. One of us thought that it would be an innovative idea to dip a finger in the sauce and put a fingerprint on the applicable diary page. In every restaurant, Phran would take out the diary, start making notes, and the same procedure was followed. What we noticed after the second restaurant experience was that the owners thought that one of us was a food critic. Needless to say, we continued this process and received wonderful service, dishes off the menu, and a number of freebies.

Trips to England were interesting, but I much preferred the seaside and country settings to London. However, on one of our trips to London, the hotel where we were staying had a casino in the same building, so that brightened my spirits. It turned out to be a private club, but I was told that as an accommodation they would issue a day pass if I had a proper sports jacket. When I replied that I did not bring one, they ushered me to a coatroom where they selected a proper fitting jacket for me to wear for the evening. Quite civilized, don't you think? I felt like James Bond. The casino was packed with people, and I had to wait to find an opening at a table game. Fortunately, I won money, which helped defray the exorbitant prices in London stores.

On one of our trips to Italy we flew to Milan, a nice city, but we could have been on Fifth Ave in New York City, with lots of designer stores and commercial areas. From there we went to a medieval castle in a small town in northern Italy. I had done research on this castle and became familiar with the various battles and sieges that occurred throughout history, so I was excited to get there. We stayed outside the main castle in the watchtower, crossing over a thousand-year-old mote and drawbridge to get there. Phran and I were desperate to gain access to the castle itself, and we would take daily walks and stop in front of the various main entrances, just hoping that someone inside would see us and let us in.

It turned out that the castle was owned by one family of several brothers, and one of the brothers happened to be taking up residence in the castle at this time. I was introduced to him and started a conversation, thinking that this was my opportunity, and as it turned out he was in the insurance business, so we had common ground to discuss. I was encouraged and mentioned to him that my wife and I have visited many castles, and we were particularly intrigued by his, and even told him that we stood by the main entrance each morning. At one point in the conversation, I asked him if his travels ever took him to New York, and he replied affirmatively. I then extended the invitation for him to stay in our home as our guest the next time he came to New York, and he politely thanked me. Now, for sure, he would have to extend an offer for us to step inside the castle. Not so much, as no matter what I tried, it was not going to happen. Of course, if Phran had been with me at that moment she would not have danced around the bush and would have simply asked him to show us the castle. Our styles were completely different, but she was the one who always accomplished the mission.

Phran and I were opposites in every way. I am a pacifist by nature who dislikes and avoids confrontation, while Phran is a warrior who never misses an opportunity to educate others about what she knows to be just and right. It was a continuous source of friction between us over the years, as finding middle ground was a challenging task. Fortunately, the love we had for each other was enough to keep us together despite the arguments and difference in approaches to the obstacles that we faced.

During the same extended trip, we were invited to spend the week in a Tuscany villa by cousin Ducky, who was celebrating his sixtieth birthday. There were lots of friends and relatives on hand, and we totaled sixteen guests. It was a large villa with comfortable rooms for all and sitting under the olive trees and lounging in the infinity pool was not hard to take. One night we decided to all go out for dinner (as opposed to the estate owner cooking for us), and the restaurant selected was about an hour's drive through the winding mountain roads. I had a rental car, Ducky had a van, and another guest also had a car, and the three vehicles would be enough to transport everyone. We formed a caravan and headed out. When we were about ten minutes from the restaurant, Ducky noticed that he needed gas, and we followed him to a rest stop that had fuel and waited patiently as he filled the tank. After we pulled back out onto the highway, we saw smoke pouring out of Ducky's van, as he had accidentally filled a vehicle that took regular gas with diesel fuel. The engine seized, and here we were, helpless tourists on the side of the road. The remaining two cars took people to the restaurant, figuring that I would return to the scene to transport the next load of people. When we arrived at the restaurant we told our plight to the owner, who immediately said that he had a solution. He would send someone to pick up the rest of the stranded people, and his friend was a mechanic, whom he would send to tow the damaged vehicle back to his repair shop. And, if we all stayed until the restaurant closed, he would make the hour drive with us to return to the villa.

We stayed as directed, enjoyed a great meal, and as promised he loaded his car to make the drive home. He knew the roads like the back of his hand, so he took the lead in the journey. I was the last car, and since there was no GPS that was working, I really did not want to get separated from the group. The lead car was taking severe curves at what had to be ninety miles per hour. I was no stranger to speed, but this was ridiculous, especially considering the total darkness and narrow roads, and I was sweating but managed to keep up. When we arrived back at the villa the owner remarked that we would have arrived fifteen minutes earlier, but the slow poke in the rear could not keep up. That was me. Reflecting on the experience, it was a stark contrast to what would have happened in New York. A person that we never met, after working a long day and evening, offers to drive more than an hour to get us home. It was an unbelievable display of human generosity and selflessness. We offered to pay him for his time, but of course he refused to accept any payment and said that he was happy to help us. Two days later we returned to the repair shop to pick up the rental van, fully expecting a bill of somewhere in the range of $2,500. The bill came to less than $500, and that included a full tank of fuel.

THE MOURNING YEARS

After Bailey's passing our home became very dark, as parts of us were gone, and getting through each day was a monumental task. After several months Jon made it all the way back, returned to college, and Phran and I were left to try to find a way to survive the loss, each of us grieving differently. Phran felt comfort sitting in Bailey's room, and I could not bear it, but once forced myself to join her. We cried and wailed until our tears ran dry, and I did not step back into her room for many years. That's the strange thing about grief. There is no right or wrong, and what brings comfort to some is torturous to others.

One morning, now out of shock and firmly ensconced in complete devastation, I suddenly remembered the early morning hours of the day of the accident. I wondered how Phran could possibly have known, but clearly, she did. From that point on I became obsessed with finding out *how* she knew. In my mind, even though I did not believe in phenomena that defied mainstream science, there were two possible explanations. Either Phran had a precognitive experience where she caught a glimpse of the future, or someone was sending her a message. Furthermore, if it were a warning, that message could have come from someone that was alive or dead.

I started meeting with medical doctors and scientists who studied consciousness, trying to determine if there were well credentialed people who had any tangible evidence that our minds could act independently of our brains. At the same time, I read incessantly, and devoured hundreds of books that deal with consciousness, extra-sensory perception, near death experiences, mediumship, reincarnation, after death communications, religion, philosophy, and physics, just to name a few categories. What I found was astounding, evidence that was more than compelling yet remained ignored by mainstream science. Reading about these things, along with my discussions with scientists, gave me hope, but the grief remained crushing. I found a grief support group that was only for parents who had lost children, and Phran and I decided to go. Every time that one of us would bring up the subject of life after physical death, the group moderator would interrupt and caution us that "We do not discuss such things here." We both thought that to be odd, because that subject is about all the parents wanted to discuss. So, instead we gathered in the parking lot with other parents after the meeting was over, sometimes freezing our asses off, talking about the evidence.

Reading and talking to Scientists gave me brief glimmers of hope, but the reality of my situation was sometimes more than I could bear. I tried going to a grief counselor, even though I doubted it would be of any help. The therapist was warm and comforting, and very interested in the exploration that I was doing related to life after death. I went to one of our scheduled appointments and found the door locked, as either I or the therapist penciled in the wrong day. So that she knew that I was there, I slid a book under her door, a book of essays, short stories and poetry written by Bailey. That evening I played back my phone messages and listened to my frazzled therapist telling me that she needed to speak with me as soon as possible. Her voice sounded weird, as it was both energetic and fearful. She also let me know that our scheduled appointment was the next day at 9:00AM.

When I arrived at the appointment, she wasted no time and began telling me what happened. She had the previous day's appointment scheduled for 11AM, instead of 9AM. She saw the book that I left, and now having an empty time slot she sat down in her chair and began reading. She came upon a passage in an essay that Bailey wrote in which she referred to me as her hero. As soon as she read that sentence, the lights in her office began flickering on and off and continued to do so for an extended period. She thought this to be strange, as the weather was perfect, the lights were fine in her waiting room, and this had never happened in the years she occupied this office space. She returned to her chair and resumed reading, and thirty seconds later her office phone rang. She answered the phone and heard a young girl giggling. The therapist asked who was speaking, but only the giggling continued. It lasted about a minute and then stopped and the line disconnected. She was convinced that this was an after-death communication and did not know how to assimilate this experience. I was paying her for the visit, but I recall spending a considerable amount of time counselling her. I continued seeing the therapist for a few more weeks, but decided that my bibliotherapy, the reading of books, was equally effective.

Phran was my lifeline in the early part of my bereavement for several reasons. She was having a slew of extraordinary experiences involving Bailey that I could not explain, and she had spiritual wisdom that I did not possess. As devastated as she was by the loss, she spent a great amount of time pulling me out of my deep chasms of despair. I realize now how extraordinary she was, and I wish that I would have had the sense to let her know it more often. It is a fact that an extraordinarily high percentage of couples who have lost children get divorced. The trauma can have devastating and long-lasting effects that can make relationships crumble under the weight of such sadness. She could have easily given up on me, but she did not. Meanwhile, we left the house only by necessity, stopped seeing friends and relatives, and celebrated no holidays. I remember saying to myself that if I could only make it through the first year, I would be OK. Of course, the second year came and there was no difference. It doesn't work that way. My life was now totally blown apart, devoid of any meaning or purpose, and I found myself in the middle of a hellish existence.

FOREVER FAMILY FOUNDATION

After our experience with the support group, the idea for Forever Family Foundation was born. Phran and I reasoned that there needed to be a place for such discussions, private gatherings where people could attend and not worry about being judged or labeled. These discussion groups were the first service offered by the foundation, which is now a global, all-volunteer not for profit organization with almost thirteen thousand members in seventy-six countries. The mission of the foundation is to educate the public about evidence of life beyond the physical and offer support to the bereaved. Much like Phran and I, the foundation is a merging of science and spirituality. Over the years, under Phran's guidance, the organization branched out into annual conferences, grief retreats, a weekly radio show, webinars, a published magazine, a medium certification program, and a host of other services.

We started airing a live radio show in two thousand and five on a local radio station that was about forty minutes from our home. Fortunately, our friend Angelina had radio experience, and mentored us in the process. It felt weird the first time I donned the big clunky headphones and spoke into the oversized microphone, plus interviewing people in the field was a rough learning experience. After a few years doing this, we realized that we needed to reach more people, as listeners had to be within a sixty-mile radius of the radio station to listen, and we were becoming a global organization. The internet was the answer, and we started broadcasting on an internet-based station from our home office. I gradually began to get more comfortable hosting the show, although it took up a tremendous amount of time. I refused to interview anyone unless I read their book and became familiar with their work, and that meant reading a minimum of four books per month. I had books all over the house, on my night table, in the bathroom, and in the office, and I would often read two books at the same time. I quickly learned the skill of speed reading, but the books looked ridiculous with the corners of hundreds of pages turned down for future reference. Some interviews were easier than others, often based upon the material and personality of the guest. Interviewing a physicist was usually harder than talking to a medium, and although some guests would never stop talking, it was like pulling teeth for others who preferred one-word answers. The radio show continues to this day, but with five different formats and more hosts.

Starting an organization from scratch is challenging enough, but the subject matter that we explored made it that much harder. People tend to be entrenched in their own belief systems, and challenging their beliefs is often seen as a threat. Of course, we were simply trying to open minds by presenting information and evidence, and not trying to convince anyone, but nonetheless we were often ignored or challenged. Such opposition often came from people who had strong religious convictions, as they were taught to believe that our work violated rules and dogma.

Phran would work eighteen-hour days running the foundation, and I would join her after coming home from my day job. Forever Family Foundation became her life, and it was as if this was something that she was destined to do. She protected and nurtured the foundation as if it was her child, and used all her skills, including her MBA, to ensure that the foundation would reach as many people as possible and thrive. In our home office, Phran's desk, as well as the entire large room, was surrounded by stacks of folders, and she used to say, "My piles have piles." However, if the phone rang and the person calling was in need, everything came to a halt as she would talk to the person for hours if necessary. I remember the phone ringing one night and when Phran answered the phone she could only make out a soft whisper on the other end, and

Phran soon realized why she was having so much trouble hearing the voice. The woman lived in the "Bible Belt", and even though she craved information about life after death, she felt that she would be in deep trouble if anyone else in her family heard this conversation. However, by the end of the conversation the woman was eternally grateful for the information the Phran provided.

We also found that many did not understand what the foundation did, and a common misconception was that we were an organization of mediums. One night the phone rang at 11:30PM, and I told Phran not to answer the call. Of course, she did anyways. The call was from a person who said that he had just discovered his brother lying dead in a field and wanted to know if we could send over a medium right away. He explained that he wanted to know the real story before calling any authorities. Phran simply told him to stop believing everything that he sees on TV, and he should hang up the phone and dial 911.

By two thousand seven we decided that it was time to start holding annual conventions, and our first was held in San Francisco in two thousand eight. It was a large event that required a year of planning, and we had ten esteemed presenters from all disciplines of research. One of our volunteers got me an interview on San Francisco's main TV news station, and this was out of my comfort zone. I was not used to public speaking, and the thought of being interviewed on TV speaking to a large audience scared the hell out of me, but for the good of the foundation I agreed. I took a cab in the early morning to the station, and upon entering I was directed to the "green room." I sat there watching the two talking heads on a screen, when I suddenly heard one say, "And next we will have Bob Ginsberg, V.P of Forever Family Foundation, who will give us unequivocal proof of an afterlife." I let out an audible "shit," prepared to be skewered, and a few minutes later I was led into the studio and told where to sit. There were two anchors, one male and one female, and they were both sporting heavy makeup and were dressed impeccably. Each of them had a set of index cards in front of them, and after they welcomed me on air, one of them said "So Bob, what is this undeniable proof that you have?" I took a deep breath and began by saying that there is no absolute proof, but there were a great many disciplines of research that strongly suggest life after death. I mentioned some of the evidence and went on to say that, when taken as a whole, life after death is the most plausible explanation.

I waited for a reaction and then watched the other anchor look at her notes and say, "Yes Bob, but what is the unequivocal proof?" I wanted to scream, "didn't you hear what I just said?" but instead I remained calm, sweat dripping down my back, and reframed what I said previously. The interview ended abruptly after that, they went to a break, and I was politely ushered out of the building. I learned a valuable lesson that day regarding the media, and we were very guarded in selecting projects from that point on.

The next year we were due to hold our annual conference in Las Vegas. Phran negotiated the contract with the venue and the entire conference was planned, that is until Phran had another vision in a dream. She dreamt that she went out to Las Vegas the day before me to start prepping, and I was due to meet her there the next day after I finished a work project. The next day, when everyone had arrived at the conference, the news broke that a plane had gone down, and that plane was headed to Las Vegas, and she saw people around her gasping as it was realized that it was my plane. After Phran awoke from that dream she immediately called the conference center and canceled the event, and we incurred significant penalty costs. Her visions were always right, so I did not think of challenging her about this decision.

I, as well as the foundation, take an evidence-based approach to phenomena that defy the principles of mainstream science. I understand perfectly why someone would remain highly skeptical of such things, because I was one of those people for much of my life. Things such as telepathy, ESP, near death experiences, deathbed visions, mediumship, reincarnation, after death communications, and a host of other phenomena suggesting that our minds can act independently of our brains, challenge the educations and careers of medical doctors, scientists and researchers who were taught that such things are not possible because they cannot be explained by the principles of physical science. And yet, even though the evidence is ignored, these things happen every day and have been since the dawn of man.

Researchers refer to life after death as survival of consciousness, and you might be wondering what could survive. We know for sure that it is not our bodies, as that would be a ridiculous notion. What survives is our consciousness (mind or soul if you prefer). In other words, we are more than our physical brains. If we can demonstrate that our minds can act independently of our brains, we can then assume that the essence of who we are continues after our bodies are shed.

I am sure that many of you have been thinking of someone that you had not thought about for decades, and then the phone rings, or an email comes in, from that person. Sometimes we perceive things without using our known physical senses. Phenomena such as intuition and extra-sensory perception exist but cannot be explained by material science.

In two thousand five I conducted an experiment involving remote viewing, which is a process by which certain people can view distant targets without physically going there, and the CIA used a pool of remote viewers during the Cold War to spy on the Russians. The remote viewer participants were simply given latitude and longitude coordinates and asked to draw descriptions of what they saw, which were often things like missile silos and factories. The results were incredible, as the drawings were amazingly accurate and of immense value to the CIA. This Stargate Project was classified for many years, but it is now de-classified and open for review. After reading numerous books about the subject, I learned that time and space did not exist in the process, as sometimes a target drawn did not exist in the present but had in the past. Similarly, sometimes targets did not exist in the present, but future exploration showed that they were built later.

In my experiment I announced that, on five consecutive days at the same exact time, I would be drawing a picture. I asked that people, even if they believed that they had no intuitive ability, to "tune in" and draw what they see, and they were asked to mail in their series of drawings once all five were completed. I purposely would not think of what I was going to draw each day until one minute before the appointed time. On the last day I decided to mix things up a bit and, instead of a picture, I drew a geometric shape, which was a dot surrounded by a series of concentric circles.

I reviewed the series of drawings that were submitted, was not impressed, and the experiment appeared to be a failure. However, I gasped when I opened the very last envelope that arrived. The sender was not able to participate on the last day but submitted four drawings. Two of the drawings were exact, with all the same detail, including the geometric shape. In the other two, as I had read happens frequently, she had all the components of my drawing, but arranged in a different order. The interesting thing is that I drew the geometric shapes on Friday, but she drew it on Wednesday. Of course, now I had to wonder who remote viewed whom. This experience opened my eyes to the nature of consciousness. There I was, with my brain inside of my skull in New York, but the participant was sitting with her brain inside of her skull, three thousand miles away in Oregon. According to physical science this was not possible, but it happened, nonetheless. Our minds can go beyond our physical body.

A near-death experience is a term that was coined to describe the phenomenon of those who are clinically dead, and are subsequently revived, reporting personal experiences suggesting an afterlife. These experiencers meet every definition that medical science has for death, including, no heartbeat, no respiration, no brain waves, and no reflexes, and yet they describe clear and lucid thinking. Although every experience is different, some common things reported include detachment and looking down at one's body, the presence of a bright light, moving through a tunnel, encounters with deceased people, feelings of warmth and peace, clear thinking, life reviews, unlimited knowledge, etc. Many are told by various entities to return to the physical world as it is not yet their time to transition. Most experiencers return absolutely convinced that they visited another realm and therefore lose all fear of death. There are a great many cases of veridical NDEs, where experiencers report seeing things going on at other locations such as another room or building. They return with information that can be verified by researchers, information that they could not have known by ordinary means. Recent developments in cardiac resuscitation techniques have enabled reports of such experiences to increase.

The study of mediums, people who claim to communicate with the deceased, has been taking place since the late nineteenth century. Eminent scientists engaged in such exploration and conducted exhaustive research using scientific protocol, and even more sophisticated research continues today. Most researchers conclude that some people can communicate with discarnate entities and can do so without fraud or trickery. Of course, fraudulent practitioners persist and ply their craft today, and there are also mediums who have some degree of intuitive ability, as do we all, but are woefully inadequate in spirit communication. In my prior book, The Medium Explosion, I stated that in my opinion eighty-five to ninety percent of all the practicing mediums today cannot do what they claim. I based this opinion on my own data in Forever Family Foundation's Medium Evaluation Certification Process, as well as my witnessing close to a thousand medium readings over the years. However, not only are there extraordinarily gifted mediums practicing today, but the evidence that they provide can be enormously helpful to those who grieve the loss of a loved one.

Most people think of reincarnation as a philosophical or religious concept, but there has been extensive scientific research suggesting that one's soul or consciousness can be reborn into the physical world in a new body. Most of this research was conducted by Ian Stephenson, MD at the University of Virginia as he investigated children's past life memories. He investigated thousands of these cases over forty years as he traveled around the world, and he concluded that certain memories, abilities, illnesses, phobias, and personalities could not be explained by heredity or environmental causes. He also reported birthmark cases that appeared on children and corresponded to a wound on the deceased people that were recalled. His research is now being continued by Jim Tucker, M.D at the same University, as well as other researchers around the world.

Although well-known to those who spend time with and around the dying, many are unfamiliar with the fact that those who are close to death often see and have conversations with loved ones who are deceased. These are called deathbed visions or end of life experiences, and usually occur anywhere from a few weeks before to the day of physical death. Those who appear to be "straddling two worlds" have clear and lucid conversations with entities that are most often unseen to others in the room. In fact, the dying usually cannot understand why others cannot see the same loved ones. Medical doctors and other mental health professionals unfamiliar with the phenomenon most often attribute such experiences to hallucinations and dismiss them. Other professionals who know that the visions are real explain that the visitors are most often close relatives, the most common of which are mothers. They also know that these experiences are not hallucinatory in nature, but lucid communications not induced by medication, and the implication of such evidence is that we are all assisted by others as we prepare to make the transition. It is quite possible that we all have a deathbed vision before dying, even though those that are physically or mentally incapacitated cannot express this to others.

There is an impressive amount of evidence that suggests discarnate entities can "imprint" a voice on recording devices, or images on screens or other platforms. During the Electronic Voice Phenomena recording process the spirit voice is not heard live but appears later when the recording is played back. During Instrumental TransCommunication the non-physical entity can project an image that can be seen and recognized by the viewer. Such images appear on "white noise" backgrounds, such as non-broadcasting TV stations, reflections in water, and various other devices and physical matter. Like mediumship, the mechanism that allows this communication to take place has yet to be discovered. Skeptics claim that such communication does not come from the deceased but is merely a result of the brain's natural process of creating meaning out of random noise, and coherent visual images out of random patterns. However, when certain EVPs are played for a group of people, or images are shown, and all can discern the same message or see the same image, it tends to discount the theory that such messages can be attributed to brain process interpretations. "Class A" examples of EVP contain voices that are clear and immediately discernible, and some appear to be responsive to experimenter requests. In visual images, photographs of the deceased person can be compared to the discarnate images.

The term After Death Communication is broad, as people in spirit communicate with those in the physical realm in multiple ways. One of the most common methods is through dream visitations, which may occur because we are most receptive to communication during certain stages of sleep. People report being visited by deceased relatives in a fashion that differs substantially from other dreams, as such visits are clear and vivid and are not forgotten upon wakening. During such visits one is often able to speak with and touch their loved one in spirit, and sometimes information is communicated that can later be verified. Such contact is not limited to dreams, as people also report a sense of presence, touches, smells, voices, telephone calls, electrical anomalies, movement of objects, and meaningful synchronicities. The point is that, although it is easy to dismiss evidence from only one discipline of study, when taken as a whole, life after physical death is the most plausible explanation.

Mostly during the early years of the foundation, I began having my own personal experiences. I journaled a total of seventy-four dream visitations that I had with Bailey. After a few years, the visitations stopped, much to my dismay. However, for a period of time I was having such visitations from others in the spirit world. Some of these people I never knew in the physical realm, but in my visitations, I *knew* who they were. In one such visit a teenage girl appeared to me, and even though I never met her, I intuitively knew her to be the deceased daughter of friends that we met through the foundation. I knew enough to make note of as many details as I could during the dream visit, as evidence would be important if I decided to tell her parents about my experience. I subsequently did decide to contact her parents, gave them extremely specific details about her appearance, our conversation, and even their home in which the visit took place. This turned out to be a meaningful experience for her parents and for me. It reassured her parents, based on specific evidence that I could not have possibly known, that their daughter still existed, but it also gave me a glimpse of what mediums are able to do. My belief is that this girl was unsuccessful in getting through to her parents, but somehow recognized that I would get the message to them. I also realized that we all have varying degrees of intuitive ability even though we may choose to ignore what we experience. After a few similar episodes of talking to the deceased in my dreams, I realized that I was intuitively useless while awake, but for some unknown reason could receive evidential information in the dream state.

The foundation became our lives and our world, and because we dealt with people in grief every day, I realized that we met all our new friends because they were also in grief, and the afterlife is all we talked with others about. I remember going out to dinner with a couple who lost their son and were involved in the foundation. Our kids asked where we were going and who we were meeting, and when I told them their reply was "Oh, another night talking about death?" That was confirmation to me of just how different our lives had become.

SURVIVING DEATH
NETFLIX DOCUSERIES

We received a call from our friend Leslie Kean, who is a brilliant independent journalist and the author of the book *Surviving Death.* She had been meeting with scientists, researchers and mediums around the world and wanted to know if I could help her score a reading that she had with a medium in Ireland. Leslie knew that I conducted a Medium Certification Evaluation process in which we evaluate the accuracy of mediums, so I was a logical resource. We met at my home and Leslie brought her written transcriptions of the readings, and, to my great surprise, this medium had an accuracy rating of over ninety percent, which is extraordinary.

A short time after her successful book was published, Leslie met with a production company with whom she had a relationship based upon other projects. The production company had been the recipient of multiple awards in film and television, and they were interested in developing a series based upon the book. The idea was pitched to Netflix, who green lighted the project enthusiastically, and since Leslie was the consultant on the project, she asked us if we would meet with the production team to discuss our participation in the series. Based upon prior experiences with the media we were hesitant and had a great many questions, but we trusted Leslie's integrity. Phran and I met with the team for hours in their New York City office, they addressed all our concerns, and we felt good about what we heard. They let us know that they would like us to anchor their segment on mediumship and grief, and since we felt comfortable that the series would be done in a fair and balanced way, we agreed.

The interviews started in our Long Island, New York home, and we were taken aback on the first day of filming. The crew pulled into our driveway with two trucks filled with equipment and about ten staff. Directors, light crew, sound crew, camera crew, and assorted professionals took over our great room and turned it into a movie set, overwhelming to say the least. Even though we had few neighbors, I wondered what they were thinking. The crews were pleasant and professional, we felt surprisingly comfortable, and my main goal during interviews was not to make a fool of myself or sound like an idiot. It helped knowing that professional editors would take over eventually, so that took some of the pressure off, especially the few times that I stumbled. During one segment a question asked by the director prompted a few tears while I was responding, and when they paused, I turned to Phran and told her that I guaranteed this scene would make it into the film, and of course it did. They filmed in our home for two days straight, including scenes in our office and backyard. They even asked if they could film us at the scene of the accident, which was about a mile from our home. Phran and I walked around that area, in the pouring rain as they filmed, and it was extremely strange as I pondered the absurdity of it all.

We were also asked if they could film one of Forever Family Foundation's Grief Retreats in Connecticut. We had reservations due to privacy issues and the fragile state of the attendees, but we finally agreed with the understanding that attendees would have guarantees that they would not be filmed unless they agreed to it in writing. The crew arrived on Friday afternoon and stayed until Sunday night, interviewing attendees and filming presentations. As promised, they did not intrude on anyone's privacy, and we were happy that their professionalism showed.

After the New York and Connecticut filming was done, and the project near completion, we received a call that they needed additional footage from us. We were surprised, as we estimated that they already had well over fifty hours of filming with Phran, me, and the foundation. By this time, we had sold our New York home and moved to Florida full time, so we were not available, but they said that these logistics were not a problem and hired a crew in Florida to visit us and do more filming. Again, I was interviewed in our home and filming was done with Phran and I walking the grounds outside.

Eventually the series of six episodes was completed and started streaming on Netflix, and it is still streaming as I write this. Days of filming resulted in about thirty minutes of content that made it into the series, and we appeared in only episode four of the six, but that is the nature of television. I thought that some of the episodes were better than others, but overall, the project accomplished what we thought it would, opening minds to possibilities that they never pondered or to which they gave serious consideration.

PHRAN'S TRANSITION

Phran always kept up with health and nutrition and would devote much time to learning as much as possible about natural pathways to healing. When I suffered from extremely high cholesterol, she insisted that I follow a regimen of diet and supplements that she designed for me, instead of taking the statin drugs recommended by physicians. I agreed, started on her plan, and when I returned to the doctor after three months my cholesterol had dropped over one hundred points. Oddly enough, when I asked the doctor if he wanted to know what I was doing, he said "no" and told me to just keep doing what I was doing. I remember walking out of his office upset that a man of science would be so closed minded that he would not want to explore alternatives to pharmaceuticals, but that is the nature of the medical business.

In two thousand eighteen Phran began to have digestive issues, and it got to the point where she could no longer sleep lying down, as she would prop herself up on multiple pillows and cushions and slept in a sitting position. She took this in stride as she stepped up her research into possible causes and tried many different diet regimens and supplements. She did voice these complaints to our medical doctor in New York, who in his holistic practice eschewed traditional medicines whenever possible. He prescribed many different things to try to help her, but none seemed to work. Phran was not a complainer, so she simply dealt with her issues as she tried to live her life as normal as possible, continuing our daily walks and bike rides, and cooking all our organic meals.

In two thousand twenty, when Covid was exploding, she suddenly started to have sharp pains in her legs. Phran had a ridiculously high tolerance for pain, but I knew that this was not a good situation. We examined her legs and saw some red marks, and with a little research saw that this could be a blood clot situation. It was evening and we sat in our living room, drinking a glass of wine, debating whether to go to the hospital emergency room. It was a place where you did not want to be when Covid was out of control, but as the pain intensified, we realized that we had no choice. When we arrived at the hospital there were desks set up outside where Covid protocol was in place, and they would not allow me to go into the hospital with Phran, so I sat worrying in the car in the parking lot. The emergency room physician told her that he did not see evidence of a clot, but there was an established testing protocol to confirm. The vascular physician that was needed to administer the test was not in the hospital, so she had to wait for him to arrive. After several hours of waiting, the physician arrived, completed the tests, and it did show blood clots in the legs. Phran asked if this could be related to the stomach issues that she was experiencing but was told that there was no correlation.

Phran was not able to take pharmaceutical drugs, as she had bad reactions to all meds, including aspirin or Tylenol. The doctor told her that she must immediately start taking a blood thinner to avoid a critical situation. Phran refused, and a battle ensued when she was told that they would be forced to admit her to the hospital if she refused to take the medication. After being held hostage and seeing no way out, she relented after a couple of hours and said that she would take the medication, despite what it might do to her. When they gave her a bottle of water to take with the pill, she advised that she can only drink spring water, which they did not have. After much negotiation, Phran called me and they allowed me to bring a bottle of spring water, which we had in the car, to a nurse who would meet me at the entrance and then bring it to Phran. The nurse was not happy. Seven hours after we arrived, in the wee hours of the morning, Phran was released.

We soon realized that we needed to find a reliable physician in Florida, where we now resided permanently. Her symptoms continued and we needed someone to follow up on the blood clot situation. We visited a recommended internist, who listened to Phran's saga, and advised that we needed to start with a sonogram, and assured Phran that he would find the underlying cause of her issues. They did the sonogram in the office, and I was a bit concerned when I saw the technician conference with the doctor. We were told that the sonogram showed a mass in the liver/pancreas area, and further testing would need to be done. The doctor said that sonograms were anything but definitive and stayed positive. A CT scan was scheduled, and we waited for the results, which came that evening as Phran and I were working in our office when the phone rang. I answered the phone, and it was the doctor confirming that there was a mass in Phran's pancreas. The phone was on speaker, and Phran and I looked at each other in stunned silence. My heart dropped, but Phran stayed positive and advised that we would deal with this. Of course, I don't know what was going on inside of her head.

The doctor said the definitive test would be an MRI, and it was scheduled. The day of the test I remember standing in front of the walls of glass in our living room as Phran was getting ready in the bathroom. I reached my hands up to the universe, praying audibly that this test would be negative, and that the other tests were just shadows or anomalies. We took the hour's drive to the radiology office and tried to engage in normal conversation, but the stress and anxiety was overwhelming. We arrived at the office and Phran was asked to sign a document that acknowledged the contrast solution that would be administered, but it also showed the possible side effects, and Phran refused and was ready to leave. We eventually compromised after telling the technician that she would only submit to the test without the contrast, and he reluctantly agreed.

Again, we waited for the doctor's call. Time stopped as we heard the words that pancreatic cancer was confirmed by the MRI, and an oncologist was recommended. How could this be? Phran did not want to see an oncologist, as she had sat with a close friend and watched as chemo ravaged her friend's body and mind, and that is something to which she swore she would never submit. Meanwhile, our New York physician kept calling to urge Phran to come to New York to start seeing a friend of his, a pioneering oncologist who specialized in pancreatic cancer, but Phran remained positive and was determined to fight the disease through nontraditional medicine. At the same time, I could not face the possibility of losing her and was lobbying to take the New York oncologist route. I set up a phone consultation with the doctor, as Phran said that she would at least listen to what he had to say. He told her that he would use a low-dose chemo protocol, and it was possible that the side effects would be minimal or non-existent. She was not convinced and resented me trying to push her into something that she did not want to do. Precious weeks went by, and I set up a second phone consultation with the oncologist and our physician, and Phran finally and reluctantly agreed to see the oncologist.

We traveled to Jonathan's home in New York, and since the chemo treatments were supposed to be every two weeks, our plan was to commute between New York and Florida. We drove to the oncologist's office in the Bronx, not knowing what to expect, and Phran's anxiety was intense. The office was not what we expected. The staff was rude, the office itself was crowded, dark, and dingy, and the doctor who we consulted with was not even going to the office anymore because of Covid. We had a consultation with the other physician in the practice, and Phran was not impressed. When she was led into the room where the chemo was administered, her worse fears were realized. This was a chemo factory, with rows and rows of people hooked up to IVs and left unattended and looking at the faces of all the patients reminded me of the horrific photos taken of concentration camp prisoners. They were sad and withered faces, devoid of meaning, purpose of hope, and resigned to the indignities of what they must endure. In Phran's prior experience with her friend, the office was cheery and the staff attentive and warm, but this was the complete opposite. Nurse Ratched from

One Flew Over the Cuckoo's Nest, ran the chemo unit, and she would not let me stay with Phran. I was banished to the small and crowded waiting area, but I assured Phran that I would be only steps away and would check on her frequently. Phran did not show emotion, but I knew that there was terror and disappointment in her heart, and I was crushed. Nobody explained to us what was being put into her veins, and we later found out that the first treatments were the opposite of the low dose that was promised.

Each round consisted of two treatments on consecutive days, and after the second dose Phran started to have bad adverse reactions to the chemo. She wanted to stop, but once again I convinced her to try one more round of chemo before stopping, and she did. It became clear that our plan of commuting would not be possible, as her physical condition made this not feasible. After the second round she announced that she was done with chemo, and at this point it was clear that we needed to go in a different direction. We drove to Manhattan to our personal physician two or three times per week, where Phran was given various IVs and injections, all natural substances that showed some promise in clinical studies. We kept up with the injections at home, and I became proficient in administering the shots. Phran was in obvious pain and discomfort by this time, and the long trips to Manhattan, as we sat in heavy traffic, were torturous. During one drive, as we crept along, Phran stared out the window as we passed retail stores and multitudes of people walking in the street. She said, "Look at all the people going about their lives in no pain." That hit me like a ton of bricks as I realized how much we take for granted as we navigate our daily lives.

We eventually stopped all the holistic treatments and went the distant healing route. A scientist that I knew was well known in energy cure circles, and he recommended a practitioner, who was in California. He would do sessions via the phone, as we engaged in certain protocols that would help the process, and Phran had high hopes that this was the answer and maintained a positive attitude. In fact, if I mentioned anything that was negative in nature Phran would chastise me, as I was impeding the process. I remembered that the scientist who developed the healing protocol lived on Long Island, about forty-five minutes from Jon's home, and I called him and asked for a personal favor. Even though he no longer administered his protocol personally, I asked if we could come to his home for sessions, and he agreed. He and his wife were very warm people who made us feel comfortable and gave us hope. I was encouraged because, although many would consider such healing to be "woo-woo," it was based on real science and had shown much promise. This was our last hope, and it *had* to work.

However, Phran's condition continued to worsen, and her pain became unbearable, but since she could not take any oral pain medication, I was helpless in addressing her pain. About 2:00AM one morning I announced that this was it, and we had to go to the hospital to get her out of pain. We drove to the nearest hospital ER, where we waited for hours while Phran suffered. Eventually I managed to grab a doctor and told him that this was absurd, that I knew that there was certain hospital protocol that they had to follow, but we were not there for a diagnosis, we just needed to get her out of pain, and making her wait for a shot of pain medication was cruel. We were in the ER for four hours before they administered pain medication, and it had minimal effects. Two doctors finally conferenced with us and asked point blank if we wanted treatment or just pain control at this point. Phran advised that it was only pain control, and hospice was recommended.

After making calls to friends, we settled on a hospice that was near to Jon's house and had a good reputation. They transported Phran by ambulance directly to the hospice, and I met them there. The staff was warm and seemed caring, and Phran was admitted to a nice room. Hospice was the only answer for Phran, as she could tolerate pain mediation only when given intravenously, which could only be accomplished in such a facility. Normally, hospices encourage family members to be present, even allowing family to sleep there, but due to Covid restrictions visitors were allowed only for two hours in the afternoon and evening. It broke my heart every time I had to leave, but Phran seemed OK with this and knew that hospice was the only option. The goal of this hospice was to get the pain stabilized to the point where the patient could be moved to home hospice. It was so strange and sad to talk with doctors who had no interest in healing, as that was not their purpose here.

Phran was eventually released to home hospice, and we set everything up in Jon's guest bedroom. She was attached to a pain pump and there was a port in her arm where medication could be administered through an IV. Things started to deteriorate rapidly, as the pain started to intensify, bodily coordination was affected, and periods of cloudiness became more frequent. Regular vomiting commenced, and we had stacks of vomit bags next to her hospital bed and recliner, which she would use throughout each day. Despite all this, Phran continued to take everything in stride. However, for someone like Phran who was known for her sharp mind, the prospect of not being able to think clearly and logically terrified her. My heart ached every time she picked up her phone and started pounding on the keys, unable to navigate emails. I spent every minute with her round the clock and I escorted her to the bathroom. One day, not realizing that her legs could collapse, she slipped from my grasp and fell to the floor. I was horrified and panicked. Even then, while she sat on the floor in her deteriorated condition, Phran was calculating the best angle of approach for me to take in trying to lift her up. She directed me to slide her to a particular spot, and then I summoned every ounce of strength I could muster to get her upright. It happened again one time in the middle of the night. Jon is a heavy sleeper and did not hear my calls, so I ran into his room to tell him I needed help, and then ran back to Phran. It was then that I hired help to assist me during the day.

About two weeks before Phran's passing she motioned me to move closer to her in the recliner. She stared into my eyes and told me that she always loved me from the day we met. She then leaned forward, and we kissed three or four times. It was a moment that will forever be frozen in time, and I am eternally grateful for her blessing me with this sacred experience.

Up until this point Phran still believed that she would be healed, and never broached the subject of her death. The pain and suffering continued to escalate, and I had to keep summoning hospice to come over to reset the pain medication dosage higher, but no matter how high it was increased, it was not enough. There was a button on the machine that could be pushed to release a dose of meds, but it was limited to every fifteen minutes. Since she was no longer capable of managing this, I sat with her twenty-four hours each day, pushing the button every fifteen minutes round the clock. Sleep was no longer an option, and my body clock reset so that I could function. Despite her clouded thinking, each time Phran made me explain what the current dosage was and how often she was getting it. Often, I could not make her understand, and she got angry. More than the pain, she did not want to get stupid, as she had to remain in control of what was happening to her. One time I stepped outside the room to talk to the nurse privately, and Phran ripped me a new one for not speaking in front of her.

Jon went to work every day, but my daughter Kori stayed with us most of the time. It pained me that the kids had to go through this trauma, but I was very grateful that we were together as a family. Five months after she was diagnosed the end was near, and Phran finally succumbed to the realization that she was dying. She went two weeks without any food or fluids, and I did not understand how a human being could survive that long without sustenance. At one-point Phran said, "I'm dying, and they won't let me in. Why won't they let me in"? When I asked who wouldn't let her in, she said that there was a line. I asked if she meant that there was a line of people waiting, she said "No, there is a line, and they won't let me cross the line." She knew that she was ready but frustrated that she was not allowed to go beyond her withered body.

At this point, I wanted the suffering to end and hoped for her passing, as we could not stand to see her like this any longer. Years ago, I thought that Dr. Kevorkian was a villain for assisting people to die, but now I realize that he was a hero. If you believe that everything has a purpose in our lives, I could not imagine the purpose for such suffering. The spiritual explanation is that there were still lessons for Phran to teach and for us to learn. I did not buy it, as I had already witnessed the imaginable suffering, and there were no more lessons to be learned.

The final act of dying was horrific, and we were not prepared. I never realized what a blessing it was for people who died quietly in their sleep. The sounds emanating from her body were nothing like anything that I had ever heard, and the gasping for air and the moaning was more than I could bear. The home hospice nurse had arrived, and she told me that, despite what I was hearing and witnessing, Phran was in the process of transitioning and was not feeling any pain. I had my doubts, and I had to periodically leave the room for brief moments to catch my breath, as I felt like I was dying along with her. The end finally came, and rivers of tears flowed. One is never prepared, despite wishing for it to happen.

After the funeral I went to Kori's home in Virginia for about a week, but then realized that I could not prolong going back to our empty house forever. I traveled home and walking into the empty house was tremendously sad. It was also surreal, as we were married for forty-six years, and I hardly remembered my life before Phran. I was now half of a person, and terrified of the future without her. There were so many things that we planned to do, so many dreams unfulfilled. Although we had not been in our Florida home for very long, we completely renovated the home and Phran's imprint was on everything I touched. I tried to pick up the pieces of my life the best I could, as I did after Bailey died, simply because I had no choice, but now I had to do it without Phran pulling me through the darkness. Before Phran died I did manage to talk to her about what she wanted me to continue in the foundation. We identified what she thought to be the most important and she told me not to stress and just do what I could. Uncharacteristically, she smiled and suggested that I simply throw a huge party, and that would be the end, but I could not discern if she was serious. Admittedly, I thought about shutting down the organization, but quickly realized that it would dishonor what she spent eighteen years building.

With much help from dedicated volunteers, we set upon growing the organization using Phran's vision.

About six months after Phran's passing, Kori called one day and told me that she and Matt were selling their home and thinking about taking a break from home ownership. She asked me what I thought about her, Matt, and my grandson Henry moving in with me. I didn't know whether this was something that they really wanted to do, or they were just concerned about me being alone, but I said sure, and they made the move. Phran said to me at the end that Henry would now be my life, so perhaps she saw this coming. Having family around me is good for my mental health, so I am grateful to have them around.

While Phran was with me I began writing a book, which she helped to organize and edit, but the book project got set aside as we were so busy with other foundation projects. However, Phran also told me before she died to "get my ass in gear and finish the book," so I made this my top priority. After the *The Medium Explosion* was published, I started to do interviews and podcasts, as this was necessary if you wanted to sell books. Since all profits of the book are donated to Forever Family Foundation, I had incentive to step outside my comfort zone and be more public. I began to feel more comfortable with such media and became good at such things, but I don't go looking for these opportunities.

As I reflect upon my life, I realize that it is not the milestone events that I treasure. Sure, birthdays, anniversaries and graduations were happy times, but in the grand scheme of things they were insignificant. What stands out are the simple moments in life where the stars align and your heart sings. For example, one time I was driving Bailey home from lacrosse practice, top down, James Taylor blaring on the radio, and we were joyfully navigating the winding road home. Trees and water surrounded us, but at that moment we were alone, together, in the vast universe. Suddenly we looked at each other and simultaneously began screaming at the top of our lungs. We then laughed hysterically as we realized that, at that moment, we were bonded forever.

Another frozen moment happened with Phran. It was her last birthday before she got sick, and we had just purchased the car of her dreams, a Maserati. People are shocked when they hear this, as Phran eschewed most material things. I still have a closet full of new designer bags in our closet that I bought her, but she would never use. However, for some reason, she loved the design of the car and for ten years always said, "Where's my Maserati?" I would tell her that the car was too expensive and about as impractical as you could get. However, she was quite upset about leaving New York and moving to Florida, so as a peace offering, I knew that we had to locate and buy the car. We celebrated her birthday by going to a wonderful upscale restaurant on our island, where we ate an exquisite meal, drank good wine, and watched a glorious sunset through the walls of glass that faced the ocean. We drove home in the new car, music reverberating through the sound system, and Phran was singing to the music. I loved to watch her smile and laugh. The drive home that night along the water was a moment that went beyond the physical, as everything, for those moments, fell into place.

LIFE WITHOUT PHRAN

Before Phran passed she said to me "Your life is about to be very different," and that turned out to be the understatement of the century. When your life becomes intertwined with another soul for so many years you identify yourself as being part of a merged entity, and when that physical bond breaks you become half a person, adrift at sea in a storm while trying to find your way through the mist.

My mother, Isabel, had died not long before Phran's passing. She was diagnosed with lung cancer, but Phran took over her care and put her on a strictly organic diet with many different supplements. Isabel responded well, but passed to spirit two years later, and the end was difficult and emotional. As much as I loved my mom, and as sorry as I was to lose her, I realized that it was quite different from losing Bailey. Perhaps it was because my mom had lived for almost ninety years, and the same feelings of a life cut short were not present. Some people asked me to compare losing Bailey, Phran, and my mom. An odd question but thought provoking. The deaths of Bailey and Phran were different but equally devastating, impossible to accept, and left me utterly shattered. My mom's passing was extremely sad, but did not consume my life, if that makes any sense.

Grief is strange. Some people find comfort in doing the same things that they used to do with their loved one, others avoid such things and engage only in new activities. Although I had not played golf in twenty years, I decided to join a local golf club and start playing again, a welcome diversion from my sorrow. The members and staff of this club must think me to be strange, as I almost always play alone and do very little socializing, although there is one member whose company I enjoy. Playing alone is a form of meditation for me, as I enjoy the scenery and escape my present world. Also, not having to compete or be judged by others results in no stress or pressure, aside from dodging the occasional alligator that decides to make your next shot that much harder.

I worked up the courage to resume the daily walks and bicycle rides that Phran and I used to take together, at first taking a different route, but eventually moving back to the same routine. Admittedly, I usually talk aloud to Phran during these excursions and wonder if she hears me. My daily activities are limited, and I am particularly good at taking extended breaks from my work in helping to run the foundation. Since sleep does not come easily, I devote an inordinate amount of time to binge watching TV, and if Phran is aware she is most likely admonishing me from the other side, as we rarely engaged in such dalliances while there was so much foundation work to do. While engaged in such activity I am relatively free from stress and sorrow as I immerse myself in the content. I have read articles about binge watching that warn that such behavior can result in various detrimental effects, including physical ailments, addiction, and other mental health issues: But what do they know? I say that anything that makes you feel better is fine when you are grieving. I once was interviewed by a psychologist, and after we were off the air, she felt compelled to tell me that I was grieving the wrong way, as filling my life with distractions is not healthy and prevents me from facing my grief. I don't believe that for a second, as I confront my own grief plenty!

I often find myself contemplating issues to which I previously did not pay attention, specifically meaning and purpose. It can be a bit frustrating, as definitive answers simply do not exist, at least not yet. Nothing can be tied into neat little packages the way I like, and it seems that the more I learn the more questions arise. I keep reminding myself to stop questioning and simply experience, as often answers come in the moment from the simplest of things.

I live very differently from before in many respects, as I no longer have dreams about the future, do not plan, have no desire to accumulate material things, and have no expectations. Whereas my favorite activity was once playing poker online, that has been replaced by, of all things, sitting on my deck and observing nature and wildlife, something that I barely noticed before. I hear the distinct sounds of all the varied species of birds and watch their flight as they whiz by at eye level. I witness the golden sun melting into the lake at sunset and the ever-changing color patterns and cloud striations at dawn, all as if I was being treated to a show sent by the universe. Every moment is either unique or perceived in a different way, and, in a sense, a metaphor for life.

The weirdest adjustment is my public profile, as for the entire forty-six years that we were married, I was always known as "Phran's husband." She was active, outgoing, and ran towards danger, whereas I was reserved, avoided confrontation, and preferred staying behind the scenes. After Phran passed I very quickly realized that, if I wanted the foundation to continue as I promised, that meant stepping into her shoes the best I could. This meant becoming involved in matters that I used to run away from or refuse to learn, which included being the face of the foundation. Of course, before my first book was published and the Netflix series aired, other than retreats and conferences there was not a pressing need for me to step out of my zone, but now I need to do what must be done. Our mantra always used to be "It is what it is," and that remains my outlook on life.

Phran told us that it would have been nice to see what our grandson Henry becomes in life, and she now gets to see this through my eyes. She told me that he would become my focus, and indeed he is my main source of entertainment and joy. I love the way his mind works, a perfect melding of his mother and father in so many ways. I try to remember our conversations and his observations, and I sometimes post these on social media for the enjoyment of others. In fact, his Facebook following is more extensive than mine.

I remain very much involved in planning and running Forever Family Foundation's Grief Retreats, but when each retreat is over,

I am emotionally drained. I know the thoughts and sadness that are collectively present among the attendees, and sometimes the grief hovers like a thick black cloud. On the other hand, I also get to witness firsthand the lightness that pushes out much of the darkness during and after each retreat. During each closing ceremony, rivers of tears flow down my cheeks, but they are both tears of sadness and joy, which is hard to explain. I know that I could be doing much more to enrich not only my life, but the lives of others, and perhaps one day I will, or not. But that's the point, we do what we can, when we feel able, and live each day as it comes. If tomorrow does not come for me, I have no regrets, and will simply experience what comes next.

HURRICANE IAN

In the middle of authoring this book we saw that a large hurricane was approaching us, but the reports showed it staying offshore, suggesting that our island would not experience significant consequences. However, the reports got graver, and the hurricane kept moving closer to the shore and growing exponentially. It reached the point where we had no choice but to abandon our plan to ride the storm out, and we evacuated in a hurry. We decided to go to a hotel in the eastern part of the state, where the storm would not be severe. Our jaws dropped as we watched the storm coverage and realized that six to fifteen feet of water would consume the entire island, and the realization set in that we could be homeless.

Our worst fears were realized, and not only did nature consume our island, but the causeway that connects Sanibel Island to the mainland collapsed in several spots, which meant that it would be impossible to get back for an extremely long time. We saw aerial photos of our home, but all we could make out was that we lost part of the roof and the pool cage was gone, but we were encouraged that the home was still standing. We also knew that the first floor had to be lost due to the flooding but hoped that the water fell short of the second floor, and that at least some windows remained intact.

Initially we stayed in hotels and rented private dwellings, as we planned our next move. I have always been the type of person who hates change, and the unknown along with the anxiety and stress that comes with it, was significant. However, when I learned that four of our neighbors decided not to evacuate and died in the storm, the clarity of perspective took over. This was just material shit, and in the bigger picture meant nothing. Losing possessions is profoundly different from losing someone you love, and the two should not even be mentioned in the same breath. Of course, I realize that the loss of one's worldly possessions, some of which cannot be replaced, results in grief that is very real. However, what I am saying is that I can look at this with perspective as a bereaved parent and widower, which enables me to better handle the situation. Admittedly, it does make me question whether I was born under a dark cloud, but I have addressed this elsewhere in this book.

Sanibel announced that they would start allowing residents to return to the island, if they could find a boat, and on the condition that you did so at your own peril. My son-in-law Matt and I chartered a boat to take us to the island, and we did so with much anticipation, as we did not know what we would find. The boat let us off on a beach about one and a half miles from our home, so we started the walk carrying the supplies that we scrounged together. The walk was a surreal experience as we moved through what looked like a war zone, no people, an eerie silence, and dead fish covering the pavement. The birds were no longer singing, and I did not know if they still existed. There was a stillness that I never experienced before, strange but at the same time thrilling in a weird sort of way, as it was as if we were exploring a new world, vaguely familiar yet quite different. We saw houses that were fully or partially collapsed, others had no roofs, and house contents and cars thrown great distances from where they originated. We saw at least one house that was burnt to the ground, and to our amazement the only thing that remained were the two garage doors, still standing erect in defiance. What also stood out is that all the trees that were not palm trees, despite their size, were uprooted. The palm trees, however, had no leaves but remained standing, the sole survivors, as if they stood guard of the neighborhood.

As we saw our home in the distance, it was still standing, a good thing. Part of the roof was gone, the pool cage lay in a heap of twisted metal, all the railings on second floor decks were gone, the soffits and fascia were gone, the pool was brown and populated by fish and debris, and the upstairs gas grill lay on the ground with all the other debris. We entered the first floor, and our worst fears were realized. The water surge reached a height of six feet, nothing was where we left it, and the first floor was a total loss. It is a large area that housed our office, rec area/TV room, kitchen, all our storage, garage, and elevator. What bothers me the most is that all my personal and foundation files are lost, as well as generations of photos and memorabilia. Matt and I worked till we dropped, mucking mud, and carrying everything that we could manage out to the curb. Darkness started to roll in, we barely made a dent, and we never got to begin the process of ripping out all the sheetrock and insulation, which is an immense job. Since there was no electricity on the island, no running water, and the bridge to the island was out, there was no way for contractors and insurance adjusters to visit.

We lost track of time and missed our boat back to the mainland, so we had to spend the night in the house. I surrounded myself with scented candles to mitigate the horrific smell that permeated the home. We found a boat back early the next day, as our bodies and minds simply had had enough. Virtually everyone on the island was in the same predicament, which was oddly comforting in the sense that we were not alone, and there might be truth to the old saying that misery loves company. However, I was struck by how upbeat everyone that I encountered remained, and how they showed compassion and desire to help their neighbors whenever possible.

One of the only things that survived the destruction of my home was a leather-bound journal. I discovered the journal last year and gave it to Kori to read, a diary that Phran kept chronicling the castle trip that we made in nineteen ninety-three in four countries and ended with visits to London and Paris. After reading the journal Kori placed it on her desk, and apparently, as the desk floated around the room, it never turned over and the papers on it stayed relatively dry. I was so happy to rediscover this, especially while finishing this book, as my long-term memory is not particularly good. Here is one of Phran's entries during our hotel stay in Paris:

"After I finished dressing for dinner, Bob got up to dress as well, and as he stood up, I noticed a Big Brown stain on the butt of his striped underwear! I couldn't stop laughing enough to explain, and I could only point. After his first glance down at his butt his facial expression was that of a senile old man who couldn't remember when it was that he had shit in his pants. However, the melted chocolate bar on the bed where he had been lounging explained it all"

I have suffered true tragedy in my life, and this pales in comparison, as things are just things. There is a profound difference between grieving the loss of material possessions that can be eventually replaced and mourning the loss of a loved one that you know you will not ever see again in the physical. With material possessions you can focus on the end result of being made whole again, so you can envision the proverbial light at the end of the tunnel. Faced with the loss of a loved one, it is exceedingly difficult to envision this light, as we think only in physical terms. It is a fact that in the material world we will never be made whole again from losing a loved one. However, if we can get to the point where we know that we will see them again in the non-physical realm and recognize that they remain very much alive in another dimension, that light comes into focus. There is one common thread to both types of losses. We see normal life continuing for all who surround us, and we question how that can be when our world is shattered or totally disrupted. Grief and trauma force us to recognize how much we take for granted in our lives, as we now see that some seemingly insignificant things are true blessings to be treasured. We have all heard the expression "you can't take it with you," which we usually dismiss, but I urge you to think deeply about this. Material possessions are just things, temporary illusions of permanence, and mean nothing. The only thing that matters in this continuum of life, the only *possessions* that you take with you, are thoughts and emotions. And the strongest of emotions are love, compassion, and empathy, all the forces that bind you to your loved ones forever.

THE NEXT CHAPTER

Our foundation Executive Board was pressuring me to agree to go back to hosting annual conferences, something that we did for many years, and my friend in Las Vegas urged me to return to his city to hold the conference that we planned years ago. I thought about Phran's vision, and the fact that we once canceled a conference there, but I reasoned that I would not be in danger now because the circumstances had changed. Besides, I now had no fear of death. I agreed to hold the conference, venues were settled upon, and planning begun.

It was time to travel to the event, and I boarded my flight the day before the conference was to begin, with anxiety about facing yet another large event. I treated myself to first class, and the trip was going smoothly, perhaps due to the single malt scotch that sat next to me. We were about an hour from our destination when I heard a loud bang that appeared to come from the right side of the plane. Despite being a seasoned traveler and used to all sorts of unusual sounds that sometimes happened during flight, I knew that this was unusual. We were nowhere near landing, so I knew that it was not an issue with a stuck landing gear. The flight attendants did not seem concerned, as the bang was not accompanied by any sudden movements of the plane, but a couple of minutes later one of the pilots exited the cockpit and looked outside one of the passenger windows, never a good sign. The pilot said nothing and simply returned to the cockpit, and minutes later one of the pilots made an announcement over the PA system. In a calm voice we were told that one of the engines had exploded, but the aircraft was well equipped to manage such an event, and we would be making an emergency landing at the closest airport. I looked out the passenger window and there were no flames coming out of the engine that I could see.

The next thing that happened was another explosion, but this time the plane took a sharp dive, the kind that made you panic on a steep roller coaster, except on a roller coaster you knew that you would be safe at the end. Panic started to set in among the passengers, and moans and shrieks were heard cascading throughout the plane. The plane managed to level off, but this time there was no announcement from the pilots. The co-pilot then came into the main cabin, looked out the other side of the plane, and rushed back to his position. The announcement came that we had now lost a second engine, passengers should be sure they are buckled, and we should listen closely to further instructions. This was not good. It is one thing to intellectualize the fact that you do not fear death, but raw emotions take over in such a situation. A strange calm came over me as I reflected upon Phran's vision and realized the irony of the situation, as despite all the reasons that I never should have booked this event in Las Vegas, I still did not listen. Phran must have been so disappointed in me from the afterlife, as once again I did not trust her instincts, despite the evidence. What a schmuck I was.

Ten minutes later we were spiraling out of control, and this time I knew the end was fast approaching. The back of my head was implanted in the back of my seat with such pressure that I wondered if it would be my head or the chair that would break first. I managed to glance out the window and saw the ground approaching at lightning speed, and in that moment I realized that I was not seeing a movie reel of my entire life, as some have described when believing that they were about to die. I also don't remember the actual impact as we crashed. My body disappeared in an instant, gone forever, and yet I found myself to still be thinking. I was confused, dazed, and my thinking was clouded, but I was not dead! Despite having studied survival of consciousness after bodily death for twenty years, I was still surprised. The first thought was "Holy shit, I was right!" I was in a darkened environment but did not panic, as I knew that I would be shown some semblance of light. The possibility of seeing Bailey and Phran dominated my mind, but I kept telling myself not to get upset if this did not happen, at least right away. In physical life my personality was to always remain in control, and when I was in situations where I started to lose control, I would panic. However, this was different, as control was a term that made sense only in the physical world, a world that I had now exited. I traveled through a curving tube, which I can only describe as a slide in a water park, and strangely I was navigating the turns not with a body, but with my mind. Nothing was discernable around me, but I did hear a low frequency hum in the background, and not only did I hear it, but I felt and smelled it, as there was no separation among my senses. I had no concept of time so I could not tell you how long I traveled in the tube, but eventually I discerned a light in the distance, which grew more intense as I got closer.

When I emerged from my journey I was surrounded by an all-encompassing light. In the physical world I would have described it as being brighter than the sun, but here it was an easy and welcoming environment, a commingling of information, emotion, love, peacefulness, and joy. It was part of me, and there was nothing to be observed. There was no panel of judges, nor was there any deity or prophet to greet me. Off in the distance there were crowds of people, but I could not discern who any of them were from my vantage point. I knew that they were part of a loving community and nothing to be feared, but I wondered if people that I loved on Earth could be among the group. And then, instantly, before me stood Phran, the love of my life. She was embodied, and even more beautiful than she was in the prior world. She appeared to be in her twenties, from my perspective, glowing, smiling, with arms extending towards me, and at that moment I realized that I had never experienced pure joy in my prior existence. If I still had a physical heart, surely it would have burst from ecstasy. We spoke to each other now without audible words, but telepathically with our minds.

Nothing was lost in translation, and I soon realized that emotions were communicated in ways that I previously could not have understood. Embracing Phran seemed to be pointless, as physical contact seemed silly considering the all-encompassing blanket of love that was present, but I tried to do it anyway. To my amazement, I could hug and kiss her as if we were still on Earth. I had much to learn about how entities of energy and thought could have a body, and I was up to the challenge. I telepathically asked Phran if she had seen Bailey, and if it were possible for me to do the same. She explained that, yes, Bailey was there to greet her. However, Bailey now resided in a realm of extremely high frequency, and it took significant effort for her to make herself known in a much denser sphere. Nevertheless, Bailey made it happen for her, and if I were patient enough my turn would come.

Now is a suitable time to address the elephant in the room, how it is possible for me to complete this book from a non-physical realm of existence. It's not as complicated as you might think, despite your anticipated incredulity at what I am about to tell you. Our foundation had a relationship with Clark, an eminent physicist for decades, and he presented often at our conferences. I loved the way his mind worked, and the fact that the more something was outside the box of Newtonian physics, the more he was intrigued. We often discussed ways in which science could uncover a means by which a discarnate entity could communicate clearly with the physical world. Tesla and Edison supposedly set out to do just that one hundred years prior, but never reached any significant degree of success. Clark felt that they never had the tools or knowledge to make this possible, but his own theory might prove to be the missing key.

It is true that researchers over the years had remarkable success in Electronic Voice Phenomena, a process by which those who were no longer embodied could imprint their voice onto recording devices. Although the researchers never identified how this was possible, they had significant success, and people in the physical world today still engage in this process. The issues are that the recorded voices are usually noticeably short, a few words or simple sentences, and often they are garbled and unintelligible. However, other times the voices are very clear, and researchers classify them as "Class A" examples of spirit communication. I was the recipient of such communication between the two realms in my physical life. After Phran passed, a friend who often experimented with this phenomenon decided to ask Phran a series of seven questions every week. She would listen to the recordings and send me the audio files. One time she asked Phran to tell us the name of the organization that she founded, and we clearly heard "Forever Family Foundation." Another session happened to take place on my birthday, and my friend asked Phran if she had any message for Bob. In playing the recording we clearly heard "Happy Birthday." I played these recordings for Clark, who was duly impressed, but he knew that we had to take this to the next level.

Clark's theory was that each of us has a specific frequency resonance. He went into explanations of quantum entanglement, torsion fields and life forces, but the bottom line is that each of us has a specific energy fingerprint that stayed with us after our consciousness survived physical death. He went on to say that if we could identify and measure one's specific energy pattern while they were in the physical, he could develop an apparatus that would be tuned to that exact frequency. Therefore, after that person physically dies, communication could take place and be received with perfect clarity due to the identical energy patterns. I did not completely understand the physics behind this, but it sounded logical. Our foundation provided funding, and Clark set out to design and build the device. Frankly, even though I had the utmost confidence in Clark, I remained doubtful that he would ever succeed. He would give me progress reports monthly over the course of a year, and they were always optimistic, and he advised that he was getting close. After thirteen months of work that was exclusive to this project, I received a call from Clark telling me that he had indeed succeeded, and we were ready for the next phase.

His plan was to map both our exact frequencies and introduce that data into his equipment. Over the course of the next year, I would make monthly trips to Clark's lab in Arizona, and he and I would devote the entire weekend to his process. Our plan was simple, but we would not know if it succeeded until one of us died. Since all the data would be housed by his device, whichever one of us was left in the physical realm would immediately activate the apparatus and start monitoring. His theory was that the survivor in the non-physical realm would begin trying to communicate tele-pathically. Logistically, since all the sophisticated equipment was in Clark's lab, this meant that if Clark went first, I would need to spend a considerable amount of time in his lab. I was prepared to do so in the name of science. If successful, this process had the potential to change the world, and it would provide the capability of direct unfiltered communication between realms of existence.

Since you are now reading this, Clark's discovery worked, and he took my exact words, transcribed them to paper, and completed the manuscript that I had provided. We had lengthy discussions about the survivor releasing the audio files to the public, however, we decided against doing so, as skeptics would simply claim that the recordings were fraudulent and argue that it offered no proof of life after death. Unfortunately, unless Clark could figure out a way to definitively show that the voice patterns emanated from a non-physical source, we would need to be patient. It would take a generation of people to go through the energy footprint process before it became accepted that spirit communication was taking place. When masses of people get to hear direct and crystal-clear communications from their deceased loved ones, all doubt will be removed. Of course, this would mean that Clark would also need to find a way to scale this project so that it would be made available to large numbers of people, but I have the upmost confidence in his abilities.

LIFE AFTER LIFE

It is a bit difficult for me to organize my thoughts in an orderly fashion, but I feel compelled to let you know what life is like here, and I will do so by addressing the questions that I used to field about the afterlife. I am a bit ashamed of the answers that I used to give to people, now that my new reality has taken the place of speculation, but I will do my best to put the ineffable into language. Let me start by saying that, as I communicate this, I have only been in this realm for a brief period of time and have much to learn. Many people believe that once we transition, we are suddenly imbued with profound knowledge about the universe, however, we are not much different here than we were when we were embodied. Memories and personalities, at least so far, remain perfectly intact. When I was in the physical dimension, I always reasoned that it must be very disorientating to die and then realize that you exist in a realm that before you could only imagine. From my observations this is true for many that arrive here, but there are those here in this world who assist, sort of like orientation counselors when you arrive in college. We breathe despite not having a body, but instead of air we intake thoughts, energy, colors, sound, and a host of other senses that were unknown to us previously. In fact, all senses are intermingled. A few people in the physical world get to experience this by having synesthesia, a phenomenon in which they can taste and smell color, for example. Some of the people that I meet have bodies and others do not, and yet their presence is the same either way. As near as I can tell, many people, especially early after their crossing, still identify themselves in varying degrees with their bodies, but that need

128

becomes less important as they evolve. When I see bodies, I hardly notice, as the shell is no longer important to someone's essence and consciousness. When I was in the physical world I used the terms *mind, consciousness,* and *soul* interchangeably, and I was not far off, as they are all aspects of the same. However, the concept of soul remains somewhat of a mystery. I was always taught that our souls are the conglomerate of multiple lifetimes, fragments that form an oversoul in an everlasting process of learning and improvement. That may be true, but so far, I have no knowledge of any previous lives, and my memories persist from only my recent life on Earth.

As previously mentioned, here all communication takes place telepathically, mind to mind. However, what I quickly found out is that I am unable to communicate with everyone here. It is easy for some, difficult for others, or not possible at all. I am told that there must be a resonance between the parties for thought to be emitted and received. You may be wondering what determines this resonance, and could it be frequency, vibration, entanglement, or degree of enlightenment? I haven't yet determined this. However, the biggest adjustment and surprise to me is that I can "hear" the thoughts of some people in this dimension, which also means that they can hear my thoughts, which might seem to be a scary proposition and an invasion of privacy in the physical realm, but here there is nothing to hide. After one becomes acclimated to the new environment, there is no ego, desire for wealth, greed, discrimination, lust, or hatred towards others. The currency here is love, and it is all pervasive. I have already related the fact that our memories and personalities still survive, so it would be reasonable for you to question how this benevolence is possible. In my own physical life, I often harbored resentment and let my ego mind dominate my actions. I felt emotions deeply, but I would have scoffed at the notion that love was a currency. The only way in which I can explain this is that one completely flips their perspective on things once they are here. Sure, we remember all our previous faults and desires, but once we realize that there is no longer any incentive to act against the greater good, we change for the better. It is true that a percentage of newer arrivals resist this change, especially those who had strong attachments to material possessions in the physical world, and for them the process of acquiescing to the new surroundings takes longer. However, those who assist others here do so without any judgment or pressure.

MOVING IN THE AFTERLIFE

I used to tell people that in the next realm one can travel at will throughout the universe simply by the process of thought. Well, it's not that simple. I previously thought of movement as going from point A to point B in a linear fashion. We decided on a destination, may have made stops along the way, and eventually arrived at our intended spot at a pre-determined time. However, here there are no such things as time and space, for they are physical terms created in a world governed by physical laws. Past, present, and future appear to coexist simultaneously, and somehow that does not seem to be weird at all, as it is all happening in the *now*. Here one needs to manipulate energy and mind to manifest desired intention, and I only describe such a process as a natural flow as opposed to a process. Remember, consciousness is made of thought patterns that flow outward through space towards where your attention is focused.

I wanted to test out this mind travel for myself, but what destination would I focus on? I have three hundred and sixty-five degree vision, but up to this point I had not ventured beyond my immediate surroundings, and I wanted to know what lay beyond. I did see vistas and landscapes, all with colors unknown to the physical world, and so vibrant were they that they were alive. There were flowers, trees, hills, mountains, buildings, and a shimmering sky within my purview, and I wondered if the others experienced what I saw. There were always people off in a distance, but they never approached, and I decided that my first thought destination would be to visit the souls who surrounded the perimeter of my world. I selected a target in this perimeter and set my intention of going there. Instantly, a group of people surrounded me, and I had no idea if I "traveled" to them, or them to me, but there was no lapse of time between my intention and its manifestation. The people were embodied, and all were people that I loved in the physical world, including my mother, all my grandparents, my mother and father-in-law, aunts, uncles, and friends. They all were young and vibrant, and all smiled and emitted a loving light. They surrounded me in a circle, and in the center was Phran, and it was then that I realized that she had orchestrated this gathering. Evidently, she got things done here the same way she did on Earth. The combined love within this circle was orgasmic, and if I had any questions before, I now knew that I was in my true home.

Two things popped into my head, the first being recognition of how silly my grief was in the physical world. That world was a blip in time in the continuum of life, and how ignorant of the bigger picture were we all. Secondly, I realized that Bailey was not in the circle. Those in the group all heard my thoughts, and simply smiled as they conveyed *it will happen*. My understanding of patience was still not complete, and this was recognized by all. Phran always answered me directly and truthfully, so I asked her what prevented me from seeing Bailey. It was then that she downloaded the information to me about levels of existence in the non-physical world, which could also be termed as spheres or dimensions. I was *born* into this present dimension, and, after gaining more knowledge, compassion, love, and empathy, will *die* in this present realm and be *born* into the next dimension. The sphere in which Bailey resided was far removed from this one, in terms of light and frequency. I would not be able to visit that realm, as it would be analogous to me in the physical world traveling into space without any means of oxygen. However, with tremendous effort, Bailey would be able to make the transition to see me, the same way that those in the circle were able to *step down*. My sense of it was that Bailey was an enlightened being, something that I intuited while she was in the physical, and I began to wonder if she would even recognize me at this point. Phran gave me that look she always did and let me know that love always remains the conduit by which communication takes place, regardless of the dimension in which we reside. One might notice an apparent contradiction regarding the future. If past, present, and future are all happening simultaneously in the now, why is it that I cannot see me meeting Bailey in the future? The best explanation that I can provide is that, just as in the physical world, some people with enhanced intuitive ability are able to catch glimpses of future events, but it doesn't always happen. Here, where it is about dimensions and not time, when it comes to observing another plane of existence one needs to raise their frequency to a level where this is possible. Similarly, an entity that exists at a much higher frequency must find a way to lower it so that a match can be made. I could not see this event until a pathway was provided that would enable it.

I decided to visit one of the glimmering buildings that sat amid the lush landscape, as I wondered how a structure, which appeared as matter in this world but was really a construct of thought, could be possible. I found myself inside a vast hall with waves of light illuminating what appeared to be a place of learning. I was not walking on solid surfaces, and it was more like being transported by beams of light. One section of the building was a library populated by hundreds of thousands of books, and they were put there for identification purposes only for the library inhabitants who were all once on Earth. Here, when you identify a book that you would like to read, the information is downloaded telepathically. What I immediately noticed when selecting a book is that I retained every-thing, in an instant, and understood the information with great clarity. As someone who read a tremendous number of books in the physical world, I had to laugh at the stark contrast to my primitive form of reading.

I noticed a large gathering of people in another area of the building that were listening to a concert. Again, I was instantly there and saw a stage with musicians holding familiar instruments. I soon realized that these props were there for the benefit of those who associated musical sound with material devices, but the music had nothing to do with the props. The telepathic surround sound was nothing like I could have imagined, and I felt myself filling with light as I was elevating. Sure, I heard soul music while embodied, but I was never actually part of the sound, as if I were one with the music.

I next moved to the art museum, where, just as I would have anticipated, great works of art were displayed on easels. The paintings were not done by masters from the physical world, but by whom I do not know. They were more like glimpses of the universe than oils on canvas, and I could hear the painting in a way that I simply cannot describe. I could taste the colors, which were different from any that I had seen previously, and they vibrated in specific sounds that resulted in a symphonic explosion of ecstasy. The painting was not a static canvas, but an interactive experience, and once again language cannot do it justice.

The creativity chamber was the most fascinating and useful experience, especially for relative newcomers like me. This is where I could harness my thought patterns into physical form, with instructors helping me along the way. Of course, I knew that psychokinesis, mind affecting matter, was a real phenomenon in my prior world, but this took it to a new level. I started with manifesting various body forms, and it was like attending my own masquerade party. I started with my own body as it appeared in my college years, but soon I was entertaining myself with all types of images and forms. I then tried an experiment, as I wanted to see if I could manifest my most recent physical body, along with the knee pain that plagued me for most of my life. I found that I could not create pain, as it was a symptom of a bodily function. Since I was now an entity of thought and energy, creating pain was not possible for me or anyone else residing in this new world. Nobody had any need for food here, but I manifested a three-pound steamed lobster, just to see if I could do it. I then took this opportunity one step further, by thinking of me getting a hole in one on a three-hundred-and-fifty-yard hole. And there I was, crushing a drive at my favorite golf course and watching the ball land in the hole. Now pushing the limit and considering that I always wanted to travel to the Earth moon, I thought about being there. Instantly I stood on the moon, no need for air, and looking at the spinning orb that was once my home. I wondered, considering the billions of stars, planets, galaxies, and moons in the universe, how it was possible for life to be only on this one miniscule dot in the vastness, but for now it was only the experience that mattered. One stark difference between travel here is that there is no scenery during the journey, which is instantaneous, and not much different from the transporters used in Star Trek. I am told that there is a way to modulate the experience by seeing more along the way, but this I have yet to learn.

Getting Through to the Physical World

The biggest priority for new arrivals to this world is to let their loved ones know that they are still very much alive. There are two obvious reasons why, the first being a desire to help alleviate grief among those left behind, as we know that the knowledge we still survive can be enormously helpful to those who mourn our passing. The second reason is our sheer awe and wonder at our new life and knowing what lies in store for them. However, despite what many in the physical realm believe, communicating across dimensions is no easy task. Some of us here find a way to get messages across as soon as physical death happens, but for most it is a learned process that takes considerable practice and mentorship.

Communications can take many forms, and people in the physical world sometimes describe these as signs. Sometimes souls in this world can manifest their energy to appear in the physical world with a recognizable form. You refer to these as apparitions or ghosts, but they are simply visitations, and nothing to be feared despite the attempts by the media to instill such emotion. I cannot tell you how these manifestations take place, but I suspect that it has something to do with extraordinary intention, desire, and manipulation of energy.

Another way of imprinting our presence into your consciousness is by entering your dreams. Sometimes, when your mind is at rest, we sense a conduit make its presence and we can enter your mind. When this happens, we can converse, hug, kiss, and smell, as if we were both in the same dimension. When you receive such a dream visitation, unlike ordinary dreams you will remember them vividly after you wake up. These reunions are the most common way for us to get through, although the process does not always work. Sometimes the conduit is weak, and we find you to be in the middle of an ordinary dream where you are rehashing events in your mind in a fragmented way that does not make sense. In those instances, the best we can do is pop into the middle of this chaos for a fleeting time, and then retreat.

Of course, you have noticed the proliferation of mediums in your world, people who claim to communicate with the dead. As mentioned, I authored a book about this called The Medium Explosion in which I stated that eighty-five to ninety percent of these practitioners cannot do what they claim. From my new perspective I can confirm that this is true, as souls here often express their difficulties in communicating through such practitioners. All people in your dimension have intuitive ability in varying degrees, but very few have the capability and proficiency of communicating with the non-physical realm. Identifying evidential mediums in your world is a challenging task, and it remains an arduous task for us here as well. I have found it helpful to set my intention to communicate, whether that be directly to my loved ones or through a medium and wait for the conduit to appear.

Mediumship takes place by way of a telepathic process, mind to mind communication. It just happens that one of the parties involved, the person in spirit, no longer has a body. However, of course our minds are very much active and alive. For communication to take place, there must be a synchronicity among the three parties involved, the medium, the sitter (person who is getting the reading), and the spirit entity. If there is a frequency imbalance within this group communication is not possible and attempts are futile. Unlike the method discovered by Clark that we are using now, transferring thought from one dimension to another is a fragile process and far from perfect. The medium, despite widespread belief, does not have a direct transmission line to the spirit world, and information received by the medium must be interpreted and translated into words. For example, I might try to send the exact same information to five different mediums, but each medium's ability to understand and communicate this information will be different. Suppose my name was George and I wanted the medium to say my name. Not all mediums hear messages from spirit, and if they do it might be received as a similar G sound, but not exact. Perhaps I would try to transmit a thought an image of George Washington, hoping that the medium was skilled enough to see that image and say the name George. But what thought image would I send if my name were Desmond? My point is that mediumship takes creativity on the part of the medium and the person in the spirit realm, so it should be easy to see that it is anything but an exact science. This is why I am so excited about the process invented by Clark as it is, in effect, a direct communication line.

Those in my dimension have all sorts of assistance from others who are always available to offer their expertise and knowledge. When it comes to getting messages to the physical world, we have what you would call mediums here to aid us in the process. As such, the communication process might involve four entities versus the three previously mentioned. We don't feel frustration in not being able to get our loved ones to recognize the signs and communications that we send, as we simply try harder to perfect our skills. Our attempts get even more difficult when the person we are trying to reach does not believe in life after death, as they tend to dismiss or not recognize what we lay before them.

Remember, not only do we retain our abilities to affect matter with our minds, but our power of psychokinesis is now greatly enhanced. So, for example, if I know that my loved one is attracted to cardinals, I will try to get a cardinal to appear before them when they least expect it. When that cardinal is noticed, people may mistakenly think that I have returned in the form of a bird, which is not true. Instead, I was able to imprint my thoughts into the bird to visit you. The same way that remote viewers can identify distant targets when given only latitude and longitude, your physical location is part of the thought package that I send. It may sound farfetched when I try to put this into words, but it is quite natural and part of the intricacies of the entangled universe.

I can give you another example of communication that happened to me when I was in your realm. When Phran was with me in the physical world, I loved the touch of her hands, as they were always warm, soft, and comforting. Sometimes while I was driving and she was sitting next to me, or lying beside me in bed, I would extend my thumb and she would wrap her warm hand around it. I did this too often for her liking, as sometimes she would say "enough already!" After Phran passed to the spirit realm, whenever I was alone in the car, I would extend my thumb and verbally or by thought ask Phran to embrace it, and I did this for almost two years with no results. One day I extended my thumb as usual and cried out to Phran that I really needed her to let me know that she was around. Instantly, my thumb started vibrating. I don't know how to describe this other than it was an energy that was constantly moving up and down the finger. It lasted about ten full minutes and then stopped. Most importantly, this was accompanied by my absolute *knowing* that this was Phran. I thanked her profusely and was incredibly grateful and elated. The reason that she had waited this long was that she knew that I was an open-minded skeptic regarding most things, and she needed to come up with a way that even I could not question.

Sometimes the signs you receive will be very subtle, such as hearing a short word or two in your mind, synchronicities, a sense of presence that someone is near, smelling an aroma, or feeling a touch. Other times it can be powerful, like seeing a materialization, a dream visitation, an electronic voice phenomenon, or a powerful and extraordinary medium reading. When I was in your world, I once conducted a survey with foundation members where I asked, given their preference, would they rather receive a communication from their loved ones in spirit directly, or through the services of a medium. I fully expected the majority to say directly, as that would have been my reply, but instead the majority answered through a medium. When I dug further, I found out that there were two reasons for their answer of medium. The first was that, if a message were received directly, they would question the source and think that it was a product of their imagination. The second reason was the fear factor, as people are taught to fear things that cannot be perceived or explained with their physical senses. Rest assured, there is nothing to fear, and we would much prefer to communicate with you directly, so stop questioning it so much.

People always used to ask me if our loved ones in the next life are always with us and see everything that we do. Although we always remain connected to you, we do not and cannot monitor your daily lives. That would take an enormous amount of energy and focus on our part, like you running the one-hundred-yard dash at top speed nonstop. Instead, strong intention and emotion summon us when we are needed. So, when we *feel* your strong sadness, love, or fear, we try to connect at those times. This does not mean that we will be successful, but these are optimal times due to the increased energy on your part.

GOD, RELIGION, AND FREE WILL

In my physical life I read extensively about people being greeted by God when they passed to the spirit realm. There were countless reports from near death experiencers that described meeting God or a religious prophet or figure upon their arrival. I have yet to come upon anyone here who had such an experience, however, I can see how one might interpret the light as the embodiment of a religious figure with whom they were familiar. That is why near-death experiencers report seeing different religious figures with whom they can relate, interpreting what they see as Jesus, others Mohammed, and so forth.

There are those here who were devout followers of different religions when they were embodied, and yet, here there is no discussion of religion. Moving here comes with the inherent knowledge that we are all one, and each of us carries what I can only term a divine spark. Suddenly the rules, dogma, and prayers to any particular God seem silly, as such beliefs stray from the true purpose of our creation. Instead of fighting over whose God is better and the true deity, we now know that love and compassion are our religion, and this is all that matters. Our self-judgement determined our placement in our present realm, and that process continues once we are here. There are no gates, no panel of judges, and nobody is floating on a cloud while harps play. You might say that our life here is not that different from the physical realms, except of course for our newly found superpowers and increased clarity. There are some here, those who had a strong attachment to the material world and their religion, who take a bit longer to come to the realization that we are one consciousness, but it doesn't take long for them to see the light. In a sense, we recognize our all-encompassing light as God.

In the physical dimension, especially within the spiritual community, the mantra was that everything happens for a reason and there are no coincidences. Now, with my new clarity, I see this belief to be far from the truth. During our earthly lives, things happen all the time without a reason. Physical life is a mixture of joy and shit, coincidences happen all the time, and not every penny that you find in the street is a communication from a deceased loved one. My point is that our physical life was *designed* to be random and chaotic. This may appear to be a contradiction in terms as the words design, and randomness appear to be opposites but let me explain.

Physical life was designed by the universe (creator, God, light) to be random. In fact, it is the only segment in the continuum of life with such a design. We were given all the tools, including the exquisite intricacies of the human body and symphony in nature, and then left alone. Our purpose in life is to recognize the true spark with us, live with love and compassion, and catch glimpses of realms of existence that are within our reach, reinforcement that we are participants in a connected universe. Things happen in this physical realm due to our own actions or the actions of others. So, when someone gets cancer, or dies in a car accident, or wins the lottery, it is not part of a plan or pre-determined. I know that you might find comfort in believing that your loved one's physical death was pre-determined and part of a bigger plan, as that can help to find meaning and relieve some guilt by knowing that it was out of your hands. However, once we leave the physical world, we then see the bigger picture and judge ourselves based upon the way we handled all the good and bad things that happened to us, including the love and compassion that we demonstrated. While in your dimension sadness can be overwhelming and debilitating, here we know that your sadness will soon be replaced by light as you reunite with those you now mourn.

Despite the organizer not interfering with the physical world, this is not to say that synchronicities do not occur, nor does it mean that those of us in the next world do not try to help. There are certain organizing principles in play in the universe, which extend to the physical world, so sometimes two seemingly unrelated events come together to form meaning. Also, as previously addressed, I try to help my loved ones by transmitting signs and communications. You might call that interference, but it is not from a judging entity. It seems to be part of life here, and thus far I have not encountered any resistance to such practice. In addition, since time does not exist here as you know it, residents of my world can sometimes perceive events that have not yet taken place in your world. In such cases we can choose to communicate a warning that might help to change an outcome. Just as free will dominates the physical world, it remains the same here. Once the physical experience ends, we can see the bigger picture, something that for most people remains obscure while immersed in the material world. I recall reading a book that featured wisdom from the world's great shamans. One shaman said that living in the physical realm was like being at a football game. If you have front row seats you can see the violence, hear the grunts and sounds, and get a sense of the general chaos. However, once you move to the top row in the stadium, you can then see the plays and patterns. In our world we have that same perspective and see that the physical world is a training ground for later examination and learning. It is part of an exquisite design for continued growth and movement towards enlightenment.

I did not go through a life review before I passed into this world, as it happened so quickly that I bypassed this process. Instead, my review occurred when I was already here, which is often the case. Recognizing all my actions that were not in keeping with my true purpose and feeling the hurt from the perspective of the person harmed, was not a pleasant experience. However, it was balanced by recognizing the love and empathy that I exhibited towards others. I felt no judgement by ethereal beings overseeing this process, grew exponentially from this experience, and I believe it determined my starting place in my new environment. I did feel guidance as I was going through this review of my physical life, not from an individual entity but from the *light*. Perhaps I had a specific guide that was part of this light whose purpose was to help me navigate, but if so, I was not able to identify that guide. The collective was more important than the individual in this dimension.

When discussing free will, there is the question of whether we can change the outcome of future events. The short answer is yes, as seemingly insignificant everyday decisions have consequences. After my children were involved in the car crash, I made a list of twenty decisions that I could have made that day that would have changed the outcome. What if I paid the check in the restaurant five seconds earlier or later? What if I listened to Phran's suggestion for her to take the sports car home? The list went on and on, and I was wracked with guilt. A few friends counseled me by saying that it was meant to happen and no decision that I made would have changed the outcome. I might have postponed it, and it might have occurred in a different circumstance, but it was fated to happen and part of a plan. For reasons stated previously, I did not believe this to be true, and I still don't. Randomness by design.

People with enhanced intuitive ability in your world do some-times catch glimpses of future events that will take place in the physical dimension. They can use this information to change the course of events, and these decisions reverberate throughout fields of energy and information. Because free will is the dominant force as you navigate your life, I would caution you not to necessarily base life decisions on information that a psychic gives you or that you intuit directly. It is not only your free will, but the free will of the collective that influences outcomes in ways that you cannot imagine. On the other hand, when you feel something in your gut and are guided in a direction, it is most often wise to follow your instincts.

In my present world, although free will still prevails, it has differ-ent meaning and is a bit difficult to explain. If I decide that I want to go to the hall of learning, I am instantly there and do not need to wait for the outcome. When deciding whether to go there, since there is no chronological time, I already know the consequences of my action and uncertainty is not part of the equation. You might believe this takes the fun and intrigue out of life, but that is from your material perspective. Once at my destination, the thoughts and actions of others in my community will affect what happens next, in the now, so there is still the element of surprise. Besides, don't you imagine that a world free of worry, stress, monetary pressures, greed, deadlines, and the well-being of others is a far better place to be? Don't get me wrong, one must navigate physical life the best they can, as the uncertainty of material life is part of a greater plan, but you should never worry about the unknown that awaits.

REINCARNATION, SOUL
GROUPS AND CONTRACTS

During my physical life I did extensive reading and spoke to researchers about past life memories and reincarnation. Out of all the evidence for survival of consciousness after bodily death, reincarnation was the hardest concept for me to accept. However, the evidence, especially from past life memories of children, was so extensive and compelling that I had to accept it as truth. I continued to seek answers to the same basic questions: Does everyone reincarnate? Why would one choose to return to a life of hardship? If we come back to learn lessons that we missed, and have no memories of what we return to learn, isn't that a futile expedition? If you choose to reincarnate, does that mean that a medium could no longer contact you? If you reincarnate to grow and learn, isn't even greater learning available in the non-physical world?

Once here I started to seek answers to these questions from those with more knowledge than I possessed, and here is what I learned regarding these questions. Reincarnation occurs but is a choice one makes after self-reflection and counsel from others, and more people choose not to return than those who do. Those who return do so because, during their life review, they realized that the balance was off as they compared positive versus negative thoughts and actions. Their return to the physical realm is an attempt to weight the scales more towards the positive. Although it is extremely difficult, it is possible to pick the families into which they will be born, but most of the time it is a random draw as one re-enters the physical dimension. Once reborn into the physical, memories of your previous incarnation still exist, sometimes with great clarity, but these memories usually fade after the chronological age of six or seven years old. I am told that it isn't so much as the memories disappearing, but indoctrination into society means questioning the memories or being told that such things are not possible. The memories, however, still exist in one's sub-conscious.

So, especially considering that the reincarnated person has no memory of his previous life after a few short years, how does one learn the lessons that brought him there in the first place? To answer this, we must first get into the nature of the soul. Soul is a term that was coined to describe the spiritual part of a person or animal, the essence of a person that is nonphysical. One's soul is their imprint of individual consciousness but may be part of a greater collective that spans many lifetimes in multiple dimensions. Since the soul is consciousness, it knows no boundaries and can exist simultaneously in many separate locations, across many dimensions. Although one may not remember previous lives, the collective soul (let's call it an oversoul) is a conglomerate of all memories of all lifetimes, a storehouse of information, personalities, and memories. Although I cannot verify this at my present stage of learning, the oversoul knows when things come into balance, and future reincarnations are no longer necessary. The mind of the oversoul tries to guide you in the right direction, even though you are not aware that this is happening.

So where does that leave me? I have no memories of a past life in the physical dimension, and I do not feel that I need a further experience in the dense physical world. Maybe things will change as I progress, but I must say that I feel that I can advance more in this realm. Based on this, my present opinion is that some people have one physical experience, and that is enough. If I don't return to the physical, there will still be a continuum and an oversoul as I continue to die in each dimension and am born into the next. My oversoul will be the same conglomerate, just without multiple physical lifetimes, but with the collection of lives in other dimensions.

The physical dimension is the only realm to which people can return. As we continue to evolve in the spheres to come, we can never return to life in the previous afterlife realm. However, it is possible to step down occasionally for a visit or glimpse, but we soon return to the dimension in which we belong.

Regarding the question of whether a medium can communicate with the person you were before your reincarnation, this should be possible. Since we are soul fragments of a greater consciousness, we can be everywhere across multiple dimensions. Even though someone is now in a different body on Earth, their prior personality and memories are still very much alive, which makes communication possible. When I used to work with mediums in my physical life, I often wondered why a medium never received information about a person's prior life, personality, and memories. Theoretically, this should be possible, but would be confusing to the medium. I remember questioning mediums about this, and even though communication with past lives never happens for them, they could not tell me why but I now see the answer. Remember, in a successful medium reading, there is a resonance among the sitter, the medium, and the person in spirit. The sitter would have no knowledge of their deceased person's previous lives or reincarnated life, so the only information that they could verify belongs to the person that they knew.

I used to hear much talk about soul contracts and soul groups. Frankly, although always open-minded, I was quite skeptical about such things. A contract is an agreement between multiple parties, and since, from my present perspective, everything in the physical world is based upon free will and self-judgment, any contract would be made with oneself. You can call that a contract if you wish, but it is more of a commitment that one tries to fulfill, a self-improvement exercise. Yes, there are helpers and guides to help steer you in the right direction, but agreements with others or judgments are never part of the process as our consciousness evolves.

Soul Group is an appropriate term, but I think of it as those of similar frequency and energy. Perhaps you can recall experiences where you met someone for the first time but had this pervasive feeling that you knew them. The chances are that you had an entanglement to that person, something that could not be explained in physical terms. This does not necessarily have anything to do with past lives, but it could. Although we always remain connected to everyone, there are individuals with whom we resonate very strongly. The chances are that when you both transition to the next world you will start off in the same realm together. My observation here is that I am connected to everyone in my realm, without exception, and my sense of it is that, when I exit this realm and enter the next, my entanglement with others in that realm will be intensified.

Despite loving our family members, we do not necessarily have an intense entanglement of consciousness with them. The love that we have for them is enough to ensure that they will be there to greet us as we enter the first dimension after physical life, but they may not reside with me in the same dimension in subsequent realms. I have a knowing that Phran and I will be connected through eternity, as evidenced by her glowing when she was here to greet me, and even though I have not been able to see Bailey yet, I know that she is part of me.

AFTERLIFE JUSTICE

Considering that a significant percentage of people in your world follow religious doctrine and believe in a heaven or hell, they may be surprised to learn what really happens. People really want to believe that the negative energies and horrible people go to a different place than those who lived a life of love and compassion.

Let me begin by telling you that people are not condemned to live a life in eternity in a realm of fire and torture. There is also not one place where others go where they merge with the divine and spend eternity in bliss. You have heard the concept that like attracts like, and that holds true here, and people that were miserable human beings that did evil things will find themselves among others of the same kind. However, remember that an evil person on earth was the product of their environment, family, culture, and societal influences. Once people are given the opportunity to experience a life review, where they feel the hurt imposed on others and are free from outside judgment, things change. Change is usually a process, and with guidance everyone eventually moves closer to the light. Remember, the physical experience is unique in the fact that most people feel disconnected and identify only with their physical body and brain. They are who their brain tells them they are, and once their soul releases from its body housing, the essence of who they really are emerges.

People who did horrible things in their physical life will enter the afterlife realm at a level commensurate with their actions, a realm that I imagine is significantly lower than the realm from which I now communicate. By the term lower I speak in terms of frequency, and I would imagine a place where their existence and opportunities are different from mine. Whereas I feel only love and compassion, the other soul may experience a degree of remorse and discomfort as he receives the thoughts of his companions. There is the proverbial light at the end of the tunnel for him too, but it will take continued work and guidance to get him there.

I have my own things to work on, but I feel fortunate to be in a world that I would term blissful and exciting. I know that I have a great deal to look forward to in the continuum of life as I progress to dimensions that will make my present realm seem primitive. I have no idea how many spheres lie ahead, or how many are below, but I feel like I belong where I am, and my sense of it is that Phran resides in the next sphere, which would explain why I do not see her much. My quest is to see Bailey, who I believe is spheres ahead and an enlightened soul. We all reach that stage eventually, not in terms of time but frequency, love, and knowledge.

I am not sure that this answers the question adequately regarding justice, but that term also implies revenge, which does not exist in any afterlife realm. There is no question that there is tremendous incentive for you to live your physical life with empathy, love, and compassion for others, as it will determine your starting point in the next life. Of course, this does not mean writing a check to an organization and then going on with your negative ways, or pillaging others at the same time you are asking for forgiveness from your God. These positive energies come only from your heart and soul, and there are no shortcuts or ways to fake it. I know that the physical realm is often dominated by feelings of revenge, as we seek to make people pay for their evil deeds. This makes sense, as we always want to protect our families, possessions, and reputations, and it is human nature to think this way. However, once free of possessions, and after you gain the knowledge that you are part of a connected consciousness, justice and revenge are no longer felt emotions.

OTHER PROBING QUESTIONS

I have recall of the questions about the afterlife that people have asked in connection to my afterlife research. I think it best if I address them individually.

Are There Pets in the Afterlife?

Consciousness is what survives physical death, and, since our pets have consciousness, they also transition to the afterlife. Various animal species have different degrees of consciousness, and it appears that not all animals survive physical death. I cannot tell you definitively how the determination is made, but I suspect that animals that move to this realm exhibited empathy and compassion in the material world, as well as the capability of showing grief. I have seen numerous dogs and cats here in my present environs. Most of these pets are attached to people who were once embodied, but not all. In other words, I have seen cats and dogs here that don't seem to be attached to people. They may have pre-deceased their owners and are waiting to see them again, or perhaps they are more, or less evolved than their prior owners. However, it appears that when both the pet owner and pet are in the spirit world, the love bond that exists between them is strong and enables both to inhabit the same sphere. What I found to be most enjoyable is that I can communicate with these pets in the same way that I do with their owners that were once human. Our discussions may not be as interesting, although some are, but these pets also exude love and compassion. Other animal species roam our landscapes, and I have seen elephants and monkeys on land, and dolphins and octopuses in the sea. I was always taught that these animals had advanced consciousness, and that is why they are here. The most interesting thing is that there is no hierarchy that defines human and animal consciousness. I was once embodied in human form, but I do not feel superior or more intelligent than the animals that are here, a place where we are all equals with the same opportunities for growth. However, insects do not make the cut, and I have never seen a cockroach in the afterlife! Since Phran and I had about fifteen cats over the years that are now all deceased, it puzzles me why I have yet to see them. I reason that they are with Phran, as she always had a stronger love bond with our pets, but I remain hopeful that they will pay me a visit.

Are There People in the Afterlife Who Once Lived on Other Planets?

It always puzzled me why a designer of unlimited universes, galaxies, planets, moons, and stars would choose to make one infinitesimal speck the only place where life existed. It made no sense then, and now I see that it is not true, at least based upon what I have been told. Life exists throughout the vast universe. It may not be life as you know it, as people appear different, but their existence is as real as yours. In advanced places, consciousness is so evolved that their physical realm is not much different from our afterlife, in other words, based totally on thought.

People in each world go to afterlife realms that are specific to the physical world from which they came, and that explains why no entity here originated from a place other than Earth. However, if Earth advances to the point where its inhabitants set up residence on other planets, those inhabitants will go to the same afterlife because they originated on Earth. Those who choose to reincarnate also return only to the place from which they came.

It is mind boggling, even for me, when I think of the implications. There are trillions of places where life exists, and each one of those worlds has multiple afterlife dimensions. Once we figure out how to synchronize disparate consciousnesses, wow! On Earth they are still trying to figure out how to get people to stop hating and killing each other, but all is one in the afterlife. I know that a physical incarnation is always the starting point and part of the design, but since all problems reside there, wouldn't it be wonderful if we could start in the afterlife? Sounds good, but there must be a foundation set upon which we can build, a place where we can face obstacles and challenges.

Do we sleep, eat, or have sex?

Since we are entities of energy and thought with no bodies, there is no need for sleep. Sleep is something that a physical body needs to revitalize itself. However, just as you become fatigued when engaged in a great deal of thinking and intellectual exercises, so do we. When that happens, we clear our minds and go within, and if that sounds like meditation, it is. Our fuel is energy and emotion, and with no physical body to nourish, there is no need for food. However, if I loved the taste of pizza when I was embodied, I might manifest one. I can then *absorb* the texture and taste, which can be quite pleasant.

Sex, although sometimes based in love, in the material world was a purely physical experience based upon bodily sensations. Obviously, that does not take place here, however, in its place we have something even more pleasurable in ways that are hard to describe, and I hinted at this when I related my experience of seeing Phran. My energy merged with hers, and as we became one it was an ethereal orgasm, more real and exhilarating than when we were in physical form. The transference of pure love from one to another is beyond words. You may be wondering, if my realm is all about love and compassion, why isn't it one big orgy? Well, in a sense it is, but not the way you may be thinking. We feel each other's love, and that is pleasant. However, for ecstasy to occur there must be perfect synchronization and a bond that transcends dimensions.

Do We Want Our Partners Left in the Physical Realm to Find New Love?

Love in the physical realm comes with baggage and can be messy. So many things come into play, including possessiveness, jealousy, family, and money. None of that exists here, and love is pure emotion. We want our loved ones to be happy and get the most out of their physical experience, so not only do we encourage them to find new love but help guide it to happen when possible. Our mutual love will always bind us through eternity, and selfishness is not part of the equation. I know that you might be questioning who you will be with in the afterlife if you spent years with another partner. Those in the same dimension are all connected, without judgment, so all are accepted unconditionally.

Do We Ever Reach Total Enlightenment?

As discussed previously, there are multitudes of afterlife realms, and movement from one realm to the next is commensurate with one's enlightenment. So, it sounds logical to me that one might eventually move to a realm in which we merge with the light and become "God-like," all-knowing and pure love. At that point, all memories of a previous incarnation(s) no longer exist, and our sole purpose is to oversee and guide others. My guess is that very few souls make it to this level, and they are like what religious folks in the physical world would call saints, prophets, or angels. Those are, of course, human language terms, but it is the closest description I can translate. I hate to use a baseball analogy, but once a Little Leaguer makes it to the Major Leagues, there is nowhere else to go. His purpose then is simply to keep refining his craft and help his teammates. When I was in the physical realm, the thought of merging into a greater consciousness, thereby losing my previous memories and personality, was a bit troubling. I now know that the reason was my inclination to think of myself as an individual entity, as opposed to an interconnected consciousness working for the greater good.

Does Grief in the Physical World Affect Those in the Spirit Realm?

This question is often asked, as people in your world want to know if we here are being held back or upset as we feel your grief. People

155

sometimes panic at the thought that they are tethering those in spirit to the physical realm and impeding their progress and evolvement. Although there is no sadness here, human sadness is a strong emotion, and we do sense that here. Therefore, we do everything we can to get messages, communications, and signs to you. However, sadness is an emotion that exists for you only, as we now know that there is nothing to be sad about. Simply put, death is an illusion, and we are very much alive. You mourn a loss that does not exist. Of course, we know that, even if you believe in the afterlife, the pain of not having us with you in the physical is profound, however, we also know that you will be here with us in an instant, even though time moves slowly for you. So, the answer is no, your sadness does not impede us in any way.

If You Have the Combined Power of Thought and Clarity, Why Can't You Help the Physical World to Improve, Like Giving Us a Cure for Cancer?

Remember I said that that the divine does not interfere with what happens in the physical world, and that is by design. However, here we do try to influence you and others for the better when we can. Although some of your scientists have attributed their discoveries to dreams and visons, you have no idea just how many of your advancements started with information transmitted from our dimension. Similarly, we have influenced musical compositions, literary masterpieces, and great works of art. However, unlike the method that Clark and I perfected, there is a limit to both our communication skills and knowledge. Once the method used here begins to become widespread, I believe that you will start to see tremendous advancements in medical science, as great minds here will be able to give intricate details to the scientists in your world.

Even if we could, we inherently know that certain earthly woes, like war, famine, mass murders, pandemics and global warning are either your own making or due to circumstance, and we cannot interfere. You evolve by solving the problems that you created, and that can be accomplished only when you return to the way it all started, with love and empathy.

Do We know When Someone is Going to Die in the Physical World?

You coined the term "deathbed visions" in your world to describe the very real phenomenon of the dying seeing already deceased relatives. To be perfectly clear, every single person in the physical realm is greeted by someone already in the afterlife realm, and it never fails to occur. When your earthly body is ravaged by disease and ready to be shed, the love bond gets even stronger, and that emotion can be sensed by your connected person(s) in our world. Most times the dying person can see us, as if we were right there with them in the physical, and that is why you might witness the person extending their arms and calling out our name. At that moment there is an intense stream of love taking place, and any fear of dying on your part no longer exists. A person may be physically or mentally incapacitated and therefore unable to communicate what they are seeing, but rest assured the escort is present. In the process of dying your consciousness is straddling two dimensions, and when this occurs your bonded people in my world are on alert and ready.

In the case of accidents where the person dies instantly, such as what happened to me in the plane crash, my greeter(s) are there when I am already in the next realm. My loved ones in spirit did not know in advance that I would be crossing over, but the release of my soul drew them to me. It is difficult to define the process, but it is a consciousness entanglement of forces that draw us together.

You may be wondering what happens if the crossing person does not know any people in the afterlife, like a child who never knew his grandparents or any other relatives. However, just because you did not know them in the physical realm, on a soul level you always remain bonded. In addition, there are those here whose purpose is to greet and comfort such souls and exhibit the same amount of love.

People in your world sometimes have strong feelings that their lives will be short. This is not because their life is fated to be that way but occurs since they can glimpse the future. Children are often very perceptive in this regard, but some adults also have strong feelings that their physical lives will be short. These feelings are often indescribable to the recipient but are sometimes pervasive and can affect their mental well-being. Once your dimension comes to realize that physical death is nothing to be feared, people will be better able to manage these feelings, precognitive dreams, and visions. However, I again urge you to remember that free will dominates, and the future that you perceive will change due to this collective free will.

How Do You Learn?

We live in a realm where there are no clocks, no time, no calendars, no obligations, no deadlines, no bodily issues, no anxiety, no worries, no crime, no wars, no greed, and no negativity. I am sure that negativity persists in other dimensions, but not in my realm. All our endeavors are directed towards the greater good, and our focus and clarity is indescribable. There are no obstructions to limit our minds and communication, and frequent discussion takes place among my brethren. Those here, even though on the same level with regards to frequency and vibration, retain various skills, abilities, and talents that they possessed in the physical sphere. Artists, musicians, philosophers, educators, and writers freely share their wisdom, as competition here is a non-factor. When a musician communicates his knowledge about music, we can see, hear, and taste the music. When a philosopher discusses deep concepts, they are not mere words, but are accompanied by a kaleidoscope of visuals and sensations that do not exist in the material world. Everything here is an experience that is happening in the moment, but we can feel what you would describe as the past and future. I composed a thought book, which was as real as the book you are presently reading. I have shared this book with others here by thought transmission, and this thought file is stored in my awareness to be retrieved at will. As previously mentioned, here books are not read but *absorbed,* as strange as this may sound to you.

Life here does not always consist of gaining knowledge and intellectual discourse. Sometimes we just explore, experiment, and have fun. In my physical life I was extremely uncomfortable with rapid descent from heights, such as a roller coaster. So, I created a mental construct of a huge roller coaster and took a ride, as I wanted to find out if, not having a body, I would feel any sensation at all. To my amazement, I did have an intense experience, but with only exhilaration and no discomfort. Since my roller coaster creation was based upon my experience in the physical world, the bodily sensations were part of the experience. These sensations were creations of the mind, and the biological reactions did not occur but only the emotions were felt. Unlike the physical world, experiences are translated directly into knowledge, so we no longer need to have reasons as to why things occur.

You might be questioning how I can grow without obstacles to overcome, as that is how learning takes place in the physical world. Here there is a pervasive thirst for knowledge, and with knowledge comes growth and light. I suppose that when I am ready to leave this dimension and become born into the next, that will happen because I reached the point where further learning can take place only in a dimension of higher frequency.

Are we meant to know what awaits us in the Afterlife?

I used to constantly hear from others that communication with the dead should not be pursued, as we were never meant to engage in such practices, and realms of existence must remain separate from each other. There were several arguments for this belief, the first of which was that it would prevent us from living in the now, learning lessons, and being the best person that we could be. Also, some believed that knowledge of an afterlife realm that was joyous would foster the desire to go there sooner than what was intended. Others argued that part of the design by the Creator was to have the various worlds operate independently.

What I can now tell you is that these people were missing the point. The very purpose of our physical incarnation is to catch glimpses of an interconnected universe and dimensions that await our arrival. The founders of your organized religions came out of ages of Mysticism, and they regularly communed with their ancestors. The key is, once you come to understand that your starting point *here* is based upon your actions in *your* world, including the love and compassion that you exhibited, that should be a tremendous motivator to live your physical life more fully. We try to get messages to you, and you should always strive to communicate with us.

Do Children Continue to Age in the Afterlife?

Age is purely a physical term used in a chronological timeline and means nothing here. Here age is wisdom, and it matters little if one spent a month or one hundred years in human form. As hard as it may be for you to imagine, I can have an intellectual discussion with and learn from someone who lived on Earth for only a year. Wisdom and compassion are not constructs of time, and a person accumulates this based upon their most recent human experience, or through an accumulation of lives. We do not see people age as you know it, but we recognize the depth and maturity of their soul as it progresses. Think of it this way: How can there be age when life is a continuum?

What Happens in the Afterlife to Those Who Take Their Own Lives?

People who die by suicide most often do so because of mental illness, depression, and hopelessness. Their transition to the afterlife is no different than those who die from other illnesses or accidents. The process of a life review and self-judgment takes place, and they begin their non-physical life in the realm in which they belong. As such, the same opportunities for growth and learning lie before them, and the stigma that your world attaches to this cause of death is unwarranted and has no basis.

Are Orbs That Appear in Photos Really Spirit?

Yes, and no. Since we are entities of thought and energy, we can sometimes manifest in physical form, and that can be in the materialization of a body form (what you would call an *apparition*) or manifest what you would call an *energy ball*. So, sometimes these orbs are us trying to make ourselves present to you. However, some of the orbs that you see have material explanations, photographic anomalies that have nothing to do with us. It is recommended that, whenever experiencing phenomena that you believe have non-physical origins, you first rule out physical explanations. Once those material possibilities are ruled out the communications can be accepted and treasured.

Do People in the Spirit Realm Remember Important Dates?

Due to the fact there is no linear time, we do not have calendars to mark specific events, so we don't have specific memories of milestone dates such as birthdays, anniversaries, dates of death. However, we are aware of such things, as we receive your thoughts and emotions. So, if it is your birthday, or the date that I was born into the physical realm, and you are thinking of me, that thought gets crystallized here. It's as if your intention collapses the wave of thought, similar to quantum entanglement. Such events remain important to us here, and we try to communicate our love on these dates that remain important to you. Also, remember that it would be wrong for you to assume that someone like me, who had a poor memory while I was in the physical, now has a better memory in the afterlife.

How Can You Communicate with someone in the Physical World who Does not Speak Your Language?

Language is a communication tool developed by man to translate thoughts into an understandable form. In my realm of pure thought, where all communication takes place telepathically, language as you know it does not exist. There is no need for translation, as we feel and absorb thoughts in a way that transcends physical interactions. When you presently listen to a piece of soulful music, you are absorbed in the moment and pure emotions dominate your experience. It is only when you are asked to describe your experience that you are forced to put it into a language form that others can understand, and often the essence of what you felt gets lost in the translation. Here, on the other hand, there is no need for translation, as experiences and communications are pure, clear, and felt. It might surprise you to learn that on Earth, before language was developed, some tribal cultures communicated telepathically. One day you will return to your roots and move closer to the next realm.

What Role Does the Brain Play in Non-Physical Communication?

As previously pointed out, our minds can act independently of our brains, and that is why we are able to survive our physical deaths. The brain no longer exists, but our consciousness has simply shed its casing and moved on. While in the physical world we are always surrounded by fields of information, frequencies, and spectrums of light that we cannot perceive with our known physical senses. Our brains act as a filter, as we would not be able to conduct our lives if we were constantly bombarded by such forces. Our brains receive information and signals, much like a radio receiver, retains what we can handle, and the rest is either ignored or put into our subconscious. When the receiver breaks, as with physical impairment or death, that does not mean the signals stop. Our minds, as evidenced by near death experiences, continue to operate with perfect clarity, bypassing the physical brain. Therefore, you should not assume that those in a coma, or impaired by dementia or disease, no longer receive our thoughts.

While I was in your world, I interviewed some scientists that did research on the psychedelic substance called DMT (Dimethyltryptamine). What struck me at the time was the fact that this substance was present in not only all humans, but also in plants and animals. I wondered what plausible reason could there be for such a substance, contained in the pineal gland of human beings, to be present at all? It did not seem to make sense considering that virtually everything in the human body had a purpose in the intricate system. Scientists reasoned that this substance could be what enabled contact with other realms to take place, and I now know this to be true. Part of the design in the interconnected universe was to have a means by which glimpses of non-physical realms could take place. In humans this substance is activated allowing certain *otherworldly* experiences to take place, moments of ecstasy, spirit communication, visions, dream visitations, and a host of other phenomena. Once we physically die, of course, such an aid is no longer needed for us, but it remains a connection mechanism for you. Also, bear in mind that you may wish to reevaluate your perspective regarding animals and plants, as we are linked to them as well.

Do People in the Spirit World Ever Get Worried or Distressed?

When I was in the physical world, much like everyone I knew, I often became anxious, worried, or despondent. It was simply part of life as I navigated through the demands, pressures, and obstacles that I encountered. I was the victim of an ego mind that was difficult to quiet, always thinking, and much of this thought was nonproductive and detrimental to my mental and physical well-being. Admittedly, there were times that I even questioned if my existence had any purpose at all. Here, on the other hand, worry and distress simply do not exist, and that is an enormous freedom that enables boundless opportunities.

In my previous world I had a good friend who gave up all his worldly possessions, traveled to an Ashram in India, and after much study and contemplation became a Swami. When he returned to the United States to continue his mission, he met me at one of our conferences in California, opting to sleep under the stars instead of being housed in the hotel. When the conference was over and he was about to embark on a walking journey to New York, I tried to give him some money for emergency purposes, as he would surely encounter periods of severe weather, hunger, and thirst. He refused to accept my offer, as he said that acceptance of the money would mean that he now had "baggage." I did not fully grasp his meaning at the time, but now in my new surroundings I see the bigger picture. In the non-physical realm there is no baggage, as such things are physical concepts based upon physical wants and needs. Such needs do not exist in the afterlife. Thoughts, energy, information, empathy, connectiveness, and love make up our existence, a life that is not tethered to any physical constructs.

Can We Practice for our own Death?

Since I have already related that the way in which you live your physical life affects your existence in the next, there are ways in which you can be better prepared. The obvious answer is to simply live your life with more love and compassion, as in the next life you will be surrounded by those of like mind. In physical life, those who feel with their heart more often than they reason with their brain will be better prepared for the next life. It is practice for a realm where ego mind reasoning no longer exists, replaced by compassion and emotion as life forces. Here, everything is an experience, and the more love that we can accumulate the better we will fare in the worlds to come.

AND THEN IT HAPPENED

My life in this dimension is fulfilling and exciting, and I have most likely painted a picture for you of an existence without wants and needs. However, as I progressed and learned, I continued to feel that something was missing, as if part of me was detached from my essence. I expressed my feelings and thoughts to my fellow souls and mentors as I sought guidance, but I received no answers and knew that only I could discover the part that could make me whole. Undoubtedly the missing piece was Bailey, but I knew from my physical life that often when one tried too hard to make things happen, it impeded the process. I was confused, as in my present world I could make things happen instantly with a simple thought, so what was blocking me from being reunited with Bailey?

I decided to do the only thing that seemed logical. Since I was an entity of thought and energy, I would simply set the intention of seeing Bailey, as if I was projecting the thought into the universe, and then let it go. I released a thought ball to percolate through the universe as it navigated the vast web of consciousness to hopefully reach its target. It was not a message born out of desperation or urgency, but simply an intention filled with love. This became a regular practice that I did with no impatience or anticipation. I knew that it would eventually happen, as Phran and others told me so, and there is no lying or deceit in this world.

I can't tell you how long I waited or how many times such transmissions were sent, as such measurements do not exist here. At one point, I heard a message that emanated from an unknown source that said, "look for the vortex." I was puzzled by the message, but reasoned that it must be referring to places in the fabric of the universe where energy and consciousness are drawn in. I could only hope that my intentions would reach one of these portals.

I kept trying to recall as many significant moments as possible that I had with Bailey when we both were in the material world. Some of these memories were a bit clouded, but others were recalled with perfect clarity. In my mind I replayed the time that, while taking Bailey on a college tour with her sister, Bailey disappeared from our tour group. I located her sitting alone on a nearby bench. As I approached, I saw that she was crying. Puzzled by this I sat down next to her and asked why she was so sad. Her reply was, "Dad, there are so many things that I *need* to do with my life; what if I don't get a chance to do them?"

After completing the replay of this memory, I suddenly felt an approaching presence. This was not unusual, as I often sensed when other entities in my world were getting ready to communicate with me. However, this was different, as I felt my energy start to intensify and vibrate at a level that I had never experienced. A *knowing* then started to surround me as excitement took over my essence. Something transformative was about to happen. Off in the distance I saw a light that was brighter than anything I had seen before. It became my total focus, and I wondered if it was another part of my glorious environment or was it something attached to me. It appeared to be moving towards me, albeit at a very slow pace. I noticed that as it neared, my awareness of my tingling increased. And then, instantly, this intelligent intense container of light joined me and made itself known. It was Bailey! No bodily form was needed, and much like when I was reunited with Phran, it was a moment of pure joy and exhilaration.

This time I felt no need to hug and kiss a physical form. Our love for each other was more than a feeling, as it was tangible and all-consuming. I felt as if I was made whole again, but heard:

"Dad, you were always whole, you know that just my body left."

"Bails, I came to realize that eventually, but until I did the pain was almost too much to bear"

"One of the purposes of life in the material world is to over-come obstacles and come to the realization that you are so much more than your physical container. I am proud of your progression, and I tried to encourage you to recognize more of my attempts to make you understand"

"Bail, did you know that you were going to die?"

"I had a pervasive feeling early on that my physical life would be short. Some people have strong intuitive abilities while embodied and can catch glimpses of their future. My physical death was not part of a plan, at least a plan as you think of it. You are on the right track in understanding this. The greater design becomes apparent when you reach the non-physical realms. I knew where I belonged in the ethereal world based upon self-examination of my circum-stances and reactions to them in the material world, the only place where things just happen."

"Why were you not here to greet me when I arrived?"

"Of course, I knew of your arrival, but it is extremely difficult for those in my sphere to visit where you are now. You needed to gain more energy and light, and I needed assistance to make inter-dimensional travel happen. The opportunity presented itself when you were able to focus on our significant moments together and the love that bonds us."

"Will I ever get to where you are?"

"Of course you will. We all do. Non-physical life is a continuous process of enlightenment. The good news is that with each death and birth into the next realm, opportunities, knowledge, love, and experiences increase exponentially."

"In all that time when my heart was bursting from the sorrow of your death, did you feel my sadness and did that hold you back in any way"?

"I felt your sadness as an expression of your love. I knew that, although you could not possibly understand, you were growing from your circumstance, and you would be better for it once you transitioned to the next world."

"Were all those dream visitations that I had really you?"

"Of course they were, every single one of them. You were a hard nut to crack, so I kept at it. I knew that you needed them, but I also knew that you would keep searching and exploring. That is essentially what all those on Earth are supposed to be doing."

"Did you really visit your old room right after you died"

"(Laughing) Of course I did! You would not take me, so I made it happen."

"When will I see you again?"

"We will be connected through eternity, bonded by undying love. I am only a thought away"

"I will love you forever, and thank you for your visit"

OBSERVATIONS

I wrote these observations and conclusions before I moved on to my present realm. Now that I am here, I believe that they have "stood the test of time" and I asked Clark to include them in this book. I am certainly not the only one who was obsessed with finding out the true purpose of our existence. Philosophers through the ages have engaged in such contemplation, and I am not sure that any progress has been made in formulating a workable hypothesis. The search for meaning often leads to angst and hopelessness, and you may simply throw up your hands and surrender to the notion that we function in a sea of randomness. It's the only conclusion one can reach when questioning why bad things happen to good people. Over the years I have come to certain personal conclusions on this topic, which I understand might not resonate with the prevailing views and beliefs, but I will nonetheless further elaborate.

I start with the suggestion that our physical world is broken. It hasn't always been that way, as ancient cultures had insights that have disappeared from the Western World. Ancient philosophers, along with mystics and shamans, tried their best to instill their knowledge of a cosmic consciousness on the masses. Ever since the trap of materialistic thinking and religious doctrine took hold, our globe has been besieged by wars, famine, greed, hatred, jealousy, discrimination, prejudice, and a laundry list of horrors that have become part of our heritage. We now reside in a disconnected world, separated by physical boundaries from our fellow man, and by conditioning from the non-physical realms.

Once we come to accept the notion that we are broken we can begin to explore the nature of our anxiety, our grief, and our disillusionment. Most of the world population adheres to religious doctrine that promises good things will happen to those who adhere to the rules. It promotes the illusion of invincibility, as certainly nothing bad will happen to us because we believe in a higher power, we are good natured at heart, and such things only happen to bad people. When tragedy strikes good people, a major complication in our grief is the notion that we have been let down, denied something to which we were entitled, and a promise was not kept. The façade crumbles as we lose our footing.

I can't tell you how many times I have heard about people who escape a perilous situation, and subsequently avow that a miracle took place as God intervened to make the save. Conversely, when the escape is not made and we experience a tragic passing, we are counseled that it was time for them to go, and God has a higher purpose in mind. It always seemed to me that such logic is faulty, as you can't have it both ways. Furthermore, suggesting to someone bereaved that a higher force neglected to intervene to save their loved one can be extremely harmful. I fully recognize that many people believe that we all have predetermined exit points from this physical realm, and that could explain why someone whose life's purpose was fulfilled is not saved by a higher source, but I am not convinced.

I do not mean to infer that religion is solely to blame for our predicament. There has been a flurry of metaphysical books in recent times that espouse the benefits of creating our own reality. Through focus and intention, we can manifest everything from wealth to happiness, and if you do not want terrible things to happen to you or the ones you love, simply focus only on the good things. I am certainly open to the possibility that this is true, however, in a broken world, the focus usually doesn't work, and many are setting themselves up for great disappointment. Maybe we only get through to the universe when there is enough collective positive energy to support the thought transmissions.

It certainly sounds like I am suggesting that we live in a disconnected random world, a realm devoid of purpose and meaning, but
it is not as bleak as it sounds. In fact, we have a definite purpose,
and we must consider the possibility that we are now broken by
design. I used to balk at the spiritual notion that our physical realm
was simply a learning experience. I didn't sign up for a lifetime of
schooling, especially when I could not recognize the subject matter
I was being taught. However, I now believe that, to a certain extent,
parts of this teaching model make sense. If we believe in an organizing design to the universe, and the evidence certainly suggests
this, then our world is broken for a reason. Once we realize our
situation, once we acknowledge the fact that we are owed nothing,
we can collectively take the steps towards becoming whole. That,
in and of itself, is our true purpose of turning the disconnect into
unity, transforming hatred into love, and recognizing the higher
forces that often remain unseen but are always in play.

We were put here to see what we make of ourselves, how we
handle randomness, and how close we come to the recognition that
higher realms of consciousness exist. There are no spiritual reasons
why good people die young, why heinous individuals live long lives,
or why some people live lives of success and happiness while others
live in poverty-stricken misery. People are often simply in the wrong
place at the wrong time based upon the decisions they or others
make, while other decisions bring good fortune.

However, the universe, knowing that this physical existence is
just a blip in eternity, takes over after our physical passing. All the
randomness suddenly becomes coherent, as from our new perspective we understand things differently. Things that we thought of
as either good or bad in the physical realm simply become experiences that have helped to prepare us for our birth into the non-
physical realm. Darkness is simply the absence of light, and in our
new environment that light can be transforming and all consum-
ing. There is one proviso, as we must be open to the possibility that
the degree of light is commensurate with our actions in the physical
realm. Miserable wretches don't experience the higher realms and

joy initially, even though progression is inherent in the cosmic consciousness. On the other hand, what we think of as angels might be the people who let their light shine while embodied.

Every time we act from the heart with compassion and empathy, we not only move one step closer to recognition of our true self, but we add one more drop of light into the reservoir of darkness that plagues our world. Our loved ones in the non-physical world may not have all the answers, but they do recognize the need for us to do our part in mending that which is broken. Therefore, they communicate and try to influence our actions. They know that when we awaken by being able to elevate from our dense environment, the barriers that shackle us diminish or disappear.

CONCLUSION

I am sure that many of you, much like myself, follow the same routines in daily life and sometimes question if there is any real purpose to life. On Earth, it is certainly hard to see the forest for the trees, as we too often see ourselves as individual and isolated entities. We stress about the most insignificant things, create fears and phobias that are unfounded, and too often think of life as a competition. We think of ourselves as our bodies and succumb to all the traps that come with that notion. What I now know is that the body is a mere temporary housing, and only when you move out of this shell do you really start to live.

You have read that my physical life was a mixture of incredible sadness and immense joy, and I imagine that many of you can say the same. We push through the sadness simply because we must, as hard as that can be. However, we also ride the waves of happiness and glee, as they are also part of the physical experience. Sometimes we just need to stop questioning "why" and simply experience.

Most parents can relate to the *why* game that they played with their child. The child wants an explanation for something and asks a question. The parent answers the question, which is followed by another *why*, and the pattern continues to evolve in a never-ending exercise in futility. We are hard wired from the start to want answers as to why things occur, and one can argue that such inquisitiveness is what keeps us moving forward as a species. If medical science can figure out why people get certain diseases, they can take steps towards finding a cure. If a plane crashes and we can figure out the cause, we can correct the problem and save lives. If your friend stops talking to you and you can find out the reason, perhaps the relationship can be restored. However, from a philosophical or spiritual perspective, asking why can be an unproductive exercise that is detrimental to one's health and well-being.

There are certain *why* questions, specifically pertaining to meaning, that are most often asked. At the top of the list is why a loving God would allow six million people die unspeakable deaths in the Holocaust, and religious and spiritual answers to that question vary. One answer often given is that all those people made "contracts" in a previous life and dying in this manner was predetermined and needed for completion of our greater soul. Another answer is that free will dominates the physical world and the event was the result of choices made by the oppressors and the oppressed. As I mentioned previously, what I believe is that the answer to the why question is that this universe was designed in a perfect state, but after creation the designer became solely an observer and never interferes. Of course, the religious community bristles at such a theory, as they believe that God is part of our life daily and is always guiding us. Physical life is random and chaotic, and that is part of the design. There is no *why*, as that infers a plan or predetermination. Our greed, our quest for power, our egoism, and our love and compassion plays a role in our own lives and that of humankind. However, sometimes pure luck and circumstance change everything. A God would not be happy with things such as the Holocaust, or the death of a child, or the daily atrocities and wars that occur, but we, both individually and collectively, make our own bed.

On the other hand, I do believe that there are certain synchronicities that occur, as the universe has a connective force that sometimes results in organization. That is why often seemingly disparate occurrences happen that come together to form meaning. I also believe that our consciousness survives our physical death, and those in the next realm can attempt to communicate and guide us. After this physical experiment and learning experience is over, we then reflect on how we managed the challenges that were put before us, and that is when everything makes sense and the why questions become clear.

We need to find balance in our lives. Some things demand investigation and a search for why they happened. Conversely, other happenings are simply meant to be experienced for what they are. In other words, there is no need to reason or judge but just contemplate and live in the moment. I don't need to know the reason that a snowflake dances and swirls in the moonlight until it reaches my hand and turns into a tear. Or why the lake turns to gold as the sun begins to set, or why a child smiles at me for no apparent reason. Dissecting such moments as opposed to simply observing and taking them in would diminish the sacredness of the experience.

We are too often paralyzed by questioning why our loved one died, why we got an illness, why our luck is so bad......all things beyond our control. There are times when we must surrender, accept, and try to use misfortune as a catalyst for uncovering our own meaning and purpose. I know that people prefer to attribute life circumstance to fate or a greater power. It releases them from responsibility for their actions and provides comfort believing that all things happen for a reason. However, as one who has experienced great happiness and devastating loss and hardship in my life, and despite all that I have learned about science and spirituality, I remain convinced that this earthly experience is a mixture of random sadness and happiness. Our purpose here is to react, adapt, and experience. The chaos ends when we move on to another realm of existence after physical death, a place where all the why questions are answered, the patterns become evident, and love is taken to a whole new level.

It seems to me what we need is a life review process that can be activated periodically while we navigate our physical lives. Half-hearted confessions about our actions, and pleas for forgiveness, appear to be an excuse for those who want to feel better about themselves due to their taking part in things that they already know are wrong. Give me a blessing, forgive my actions, and let me walk away to resume my life with little change. I can come back again for absolution, so why not rape and pillage? The whole concept is silly in my view.

Could you imagine if we all woke up tomorrow with the super-power of having our thoughts and actions simultaneously melded with the thoughts and feelings of others? Give the love, feel the love. Cause the pain and distress, feel the pain and distress. That is what the afterlife is like. You might argue that our physical world was not designed that way, as we grow from life's experiences and how we react to obstacles. That may be true, but I can't think of a better way to learn and grow than walking in the shoes of our brethren.

I think that we would all lead fuller lives if we could come to the realization that there is nothing permanent in our physical lives. Every day there are hundreds of assumptions that we make as we continuously take things for granted. We expect an orderly progression of events in our lives and anticipate that they will take place in a linear fashion. And yet, material possessions come and go, our loved ones are suddenly no more, and our lives change in an instant. Many believe, as do I, that the only constant, the only thing that has permanence, is our consciousness. The concept sounds absurd to those who believe only in what can be perceived by their physical senses. After all, a rock is permanent, and the mind is simply an epiphenomenon of the brain. But if it's not, we need to flip the switch on how we think. What if our physical world is not concrete, but illusive? What if, by seemingly faulty logic, our present lives are the only part of a continuum of life where nothing is as it seems? Perhaps when our mind moves to another realm, we can only then discover the constant in our lives. Chaos turns to order as we realize that consciousness is the ground of all being. Living our present lives with the knowledge that all things are temporary enables us to treasure what is put before us. Then, and only then, can we love more deeply and genuinely appreciate that which may disappear tomorrow.

EPILOGUE

This book is a combination of fact and fiction. The autobiographical content is all true, but the plane crash and my subsequent death is fiction. The concepts and information provided about the next world are based upon my extensive reading on the subject of survival of consciousness, interviews that I have conducted, and my own intuition. As of this writing, I remain very much alive and continue my search for meaning and purpose. We will most likely never understand the complexities of the non-physical realm until we get there. I am in no rush to get there, but I have no fear and look forward to rejoicing with my loved ones when I arrive.

ACKNOWLEDGEMENTS

Bailey, Phran and my mother Isabel, remain my inspiration as I navigate this strange world, and I suspect that everything that I do, or write, has their imprint. While they guide me from the next world, Kori, Jon, Matt, and Henry do their best to help me in this dimension. Since much of my present life revolves around Forever Family Foundation, I am extremely grateful for the support of friends and foundation volunteers, including Leigh Harris, Tom and Melissa Gould, Donna and Matt Mello, Barry Ginsberg, Dr. Mo Hannah, Annette Marinaccio, Loyd Auerbach, Dianne Arcangel, Liz Entin, Janet Mayer, Dr.Betty Kovacs, Kim Saavedra, Dr. Stephen Braude, Kathleen Murray, Arthur Perkins, Dr. Jeff Kane, Janet Kane, Tiffany Burger, Dr. Piero Calvi-Parisetti, Angela Higney, Joe and Linda Bonventre, Joseph Shiel, Dave and Joanne Kane, Lenny and Val Ficarelle, Ducky and Shorty Erlichman, Johanna Suchow, Irv Rosenbaum, Anne Rambo, Angelina Diana, and the many mediums, scientists, and academics who continue to devote their lives to help those in grief.

ABOUT THE AUTHOR

Bob Ginsberg started researching the evidence for survival of consciousness soon after his daughter died in 2002. Devastated by the loss, he needed science to tell him if she still existed in some form. In 2004 Bob and his wife Phran founded Forever Family Foundation (foreverfamilyfoundation.org), a global not for profit that educates the public about evidence that we are more than our physical bodies. Bob hosts the Signs of Life radio show, is past editor of Signs of Life Magazine, heads the foundation's Medium Evaluation Certification Program, writes a blog at beyondthefivesenses.com, and is the author of The Medium Explosion. Bob, Phran and the foundation are currently featured in the Netflix Docuseries Surviving Death. Sadly, Phran passed to the Spirit realm September 22, 2020.

Made in United States
North Haven, CT
16 April 2023

35503805R00114